BEING BENEDICT CUMBERBATCH

BEING BENEDICT CUMBERBATCH

JOANNA BENECKE

Plexus, London

CONTENTS

INTRODUCTION

Benedict Cumberbatch: a name it's impossible to read without wanting to say out loud. It's got that weird English crunchy compelling sexiness to it. Go ahead, say it right now. I don't care if you're on a bus or a train or a taxi or the end of a bungee cord – say it. Scream it. Sing it. Everyone will join in; you'll get a chorus going. Because the Cumberlove is catching. Ben-e-dict Cum-ber-batch. Bene-dict Cumber-batch. Benedictcumberbatch. Ah, it's like a yogic mantra (btw, fact fans: Benedict himself is a yoga enthusiast, but more on that later).

Let's rewind – past hobbits, star trekking, war horses and the world's most famous sleuth – back to the very beginning. Benedict Timothy Carlton Cumberbatch, to give him his full credentials, was born on 19 July 1976, the only child of actor parents Wanda Ventham and Timothy Carlton (for the purposes of this book they'll hereafter be referred to by the collective noun of 'Wimothy'. You've definitely glimpsed both of them before; they appear as Mr and Mrs Holmes in season three

of *Sherlock*!). Wimothy were obviously overjoyed to welcome their overactive, skinny little baby, even if the rest of the world remained largely unaware that a superstar was slowly rising in an unassuming flat in the classy London borough of Kensington . . .

Then, on 25 July 2010, the first episode of *Sherlock* screened in the UK – and THE WORLD CHANGED. Sporting a shabby long coat (the sort that usually causes worried parents to desperately count their children), overgrown hair (think guinea-pig-atop-head) and some sort of personality disorder (yes, we love him, but let's face it, he's also a full-on 'high-functioning sociopath' with a less than healthy appetite for deduction and occasional violence), Benedict Cumberbatch won our hearts and minds in an instant, and gave sexy a new name. (And that name sounded a lot like Bandercoot Cabbagepatch . . .)

But, of course, we don't just love him for his name. That would be shallow.

There's also that chiselled Cumber-face: you can't lay eyes on that skinny oval-meets-upside-down-triangle without wanting to stroke (or lick, let's be honest) those fine and defined cheekbones. The Cumbertones: a voice you can't hear without coming over all shivery, *à la* Sherlock when confronted with a particularly gory murder. The Cumberbod: whether Sherlock-skinny or *Star-Trek*-leanly-beefed-up-muscle, he's 6'1/2" (that extra half an inch is all-important) of long-limbed hugability. But most of all, we love the witty, intelligent, sexy Cumberbrain he's got stored in that weirdly-shaped, floppy-hair-covered skull of his. (See, we are *not* shallow.) As that lucky cow Irene Adler says of Sherlock, 'Brainy's the new sexy.' You're preaching to the converted, Adler . . . now, go put some clothes on.

But his brain isn't Benedict's only amazing organ; there's also his massive… Cumberheart! Whether he's galloping up to hug fans from far afield during TV interviews; writing politically-minded notes to the paparazzi ('Go photograph Egypt and show the world something important'); doing those modest little face-folds when people praise him (you know, that sort of chin-tuck where his neck seems to be eating his face); devoting time to charities like the Elton John AIDS Foundation; or worrying about the damage to feminism caused

> '**My creature comforts? A whisky, the fire and a good book.**'
>
> *— Benedict Cumberbatch*

by the word 'Cumberbitch'; Benedict has shown that he's far from a cold fish (despite all those internet memes comparing him to a hammerhead shark). He's the good guy who also does an excellent job of playing the bad guy. Which makes him kind of perfect.

As I am not Benedict Cumberbatch (it's one of life's great tragedies that there's only one of him), I can never truly know what it is like inside that beautiful Cumbermind of his. However, by examining all the information we have about the Cumberman and his Cumberverse we can hopefully get our Sherlock on and do some hardcore deducing. Thus we'll come as close as possible to determining just what BEING BENEDICT CUMBERBATCH is all about. One thing's for certain: it's gonna be Cumberlicious. (Oh, and there'll be hot pics too.)

What a scarf up: Looking dapper at BALLY's '60 Years of Conquering Everest' celebration, held at Bedford Square Gardens, London, in January 2013.

BENEDICT

CUMBAGE PATCH KID

'Having your adolescence at an all-male boarding school is just crap.'

– Benedict Cumberbatch

IN THE BEGINNING I know it's hard to imagine a time B.B. (Before Benedict), but apparently there was one. Actors Wanda Ventham and Timothy Carlton (aka Wimothy) met in 1970 while filming a drama series called *A Family at War* on location in Ireland. Thankfully they didn't let the gloomy title get them down and fell in love with each other almost immediately. Wanda's first marriage, to businessman James Tabernacle (with whom she has a daughter, Tracy), had been on the rocks for some time and, though she

Naturally sun-kissed or victim of an overzealous make-up artist? B'batch enjoys his moment in the sun at a *Hawking* photo-call at the Monte Carlo Television Festival, July 2004.

insisted in an interview with the *TV Times* in 1979 that, 'Tim didn't break up the marriage', she acknowledges that he was the catalyst she required to make the break. 'I suppose he was what was needed to help me make the final decision. All divorces are unpleasant, but I was lucky because I had someone in my life to cushion me.' Although she loved Tim, Wanda was reluctant to remarry given the outcome of her first marriage. But Tim finally persuaded her. 'Tim is a great romantic, which is really why – in the end – I decided I would remarry.' So it was romance that made her say 'I do'. (And maybe also the fact that she was with Cumberchild.)

The couple married in April 1976. Three months later, on 19 July, Benedict was born at Queen Charlotte's Hospital in Hammersmith, London (incidentally, this is also the birthplace of actors Daniel Radcliffe, Mischa Barton and Dame Helen Mirren. Which begs the question: do they employ talent scouts as midwives?)

Benedict Cumberbatch had arrived.

CUMBERKID

Baby Benedict was pale, tall and hyper; 'a whirlwind – he never stopped,' according to Wanda. When he cried, Wimothy would carry him up to the roof of their top-floor flat in Kensington and leave him there in his pram for a little while, as the tiny B'batch loved looking up at the sky. He'd stare in fascination at the expanse of blue (or more often, grey, this being London), stop crying and smile. When quizzed by the *Evening Standard* as to his earliest London memory, a 33-year-old Benedict didn't hesitate. 'Being on the rooftop and seeing a helicopter fly over to land at Kensington Palace,' recalls B'batch. 'My parents claim that my first word was helicopter.' Aw, super sweet! Except for the time his penchant for sky-gazing nearly killed him . . .

One winter's day Wimothy went out, leaving Tracy, Benedict's half-sister, to babysit. She took a bawling baby Benedict up onto the roof, with the intention of fetching him down after a minute or two – only to totally forget he was there. She didn't remember till she

'He was a whirlwind – he never stopped.'

– Wanda Ventham

saw snow start to fall outside the kitchen window. In a panic, she raced up to the roof to find a freezing icicle Benebaby, teeth chattering, but still smiling up at the night sky – even though he'd turned blue. She hurriedly carried him inside and placed him on a radiator to thaw him out. By the time his parents returned home, he was back to normal.

Of course, Benedict did go on to be a bit of a sickly child, having his tonsils out and his adenoids scraped at the age of three. But these operations in no way slowed him down, as Wanda told the *TV Times* in 1979 when a reporter arrived at the flat to interview her, '[Benedict] has been rather vile today [. . .] you've hit on a bad day. He has just had his adenoids and tonsils out and his temperament has gone slightly loopy in the last day or so. But even at times like this Tim is fantastic with him.' Tim proceeded to take his boisterous son into another room to 'entertain' him while Wanda was being interviewed.

Despite having a healthy appetite, little Benedict was incredibly thin. Wanda worried that her son might have

A Cumberchild is born! Benedict's very first photo opportunity, with proud parents Wanda Ventham and Timothy Carlton, 22 July 1976.

'Helicopter!' Sky-gazing with his mother. Learning to speak has never been so much fun. Back in the day, this toddling B'batch lived next door to *Sherlock* actress Una Stubbs.

Hudson in *Sherlock*. As she is an acting contemporary and friend of Wimothy, young Benedict saw a fair bit of her as a child – whether baby B'batch liked it or not. 'I did films with Wanda Ventham, his mother, and we lived in the same area, in Kensington,' revealed Una in an interview with the *Radio Times*. 'So I'd be out with my pram and Wanda and I would be talking and there was poor little Benedict – who I suppose was about four – standing there while we were gossiping in the high street for hours!' She remembers him as being 'very polite . . . a lovely boy'. Little did she know that one day he'd be playing her extremely rude lodger . . .

SCHOOL

Though the brouhaha surrounding his Cumber-heritage has never quite gone away – 'talking about class terrifies me,' sighs Benedict. 'There is no way of winning. You either come across as being arrogant and ungrateful if you complain . . . or snooty and over-privileged if you bathe in it' – the fact remains that both Wanda and Timothy were 'working actors who never knew when the next pay day might come' (that's how B'batch told it to the *Radio Times*, anyhow). But posh or not, prosperous or penniless, Wimothy spared no expense when it came to the education of their only son. 'They wanted the best for me,' states Benedict simply – even if 'the best' entailed

an overactive thyroid, as he was so stick-like. But his thyroid was absolutely fine. 'I had a very fast metabolism,' explains Benedict. And he was ridiculously active; he ran everywhere, arriving at school drenched in sweat. 'I never stopped,' he says.

Despite living in Kensington, a veritable hotspot for the rich and fabulous, Benedict didn't lead a *Made-In-Chelsea*-type existence. He describes his childhood hood as, 'when Kensington was run-down; smalls hanging out in the smog, riots in Notting Hill.' A neighbour to the Ventham-Carlton-Cumberbatches was none other than Una Stubbs, who plays Mrs

Just another day at the office for hard-grafting actors Timothy and Wanda. Here they are starring in an episode of legal drama, *Crown Court*, 1977.

'Playing a trumpet wounds you . . . I have trumpet-mouth.'

– Benedict Cumberbatch

scrimping and saving to afford the fees for Brambletye, a Church of England prep school in West Sussex. For the young B'batch, this meant leaving the family home in London and becoming a boarder – a scary prospect for any eight-year-old. But he took it in his stride. 'I thrived,' he says, even if, 'eight seems a bit of a wrench. I don't know if I could do it with a kid of eight.'

Around this time Wimothy witnessed an early indication of Benedict's starry thespian future. They had taken him to visit his godmother, also an actor, who let her young godson explore the empty stage at the theatre where she was performing. Benedict described the experience to *Tinker Tailor Soldier Spy* co-star Gary Oldman in *Interview Magazine*. 'I just remember looking out into the darkness, and it pulled me in, rather than pushed me away, if you know what I mean. It gave me a real energy and thrill to think about communicating with that, rather than turning away and going home and having a cup of tea and leaving it to someone else. And as adults, [my mother, father and godmother] just looked at each other with raised eyebrows, all three of them actors, and went, "Oh dear."'

By the time Benedict arrived at Brambletye, recent additions to the school and grounds included: swimming pool, squash courts and science lab. The latter was somewhat wasted on young B'batch, however, as he didn't pay much attention in science classes. He was a bit of a 'tearaway' in those days, he confessed in an interview for the *Telegraph*. 'I was pretty naughty, I got into fights.' The teachers responded by nudging him not-so-gently into acting and he made several appearances in the school theatre. For instance, he was in the school production of 1960s musical comedy *Half a Sixpence*, playing the lead female role: Ann the chambermaid. (Though Brambletye now admits both girls and boys, back in Benedict's day it was a single-sex school – thus giving the B'batch plenty of opportunities to wear skirts on stage.) The musical was originally written as a vehicle for rock'n'roll legend Tommy Steele. I bet he'd have been thrilled to have Benedict as his love interest – who wouldn't? Sadly there is no word on whether B.C.'s singing voice back then was as shiver-inducing as his current melodious baritone, but I reckon it probably was just as beautiful, if a tad shriller.

In other musical pursuits, Benedict started playing the trumpet at around age ten and blames the mouth-gymnastics involved for shaping his lips in strange new ways. 'Playing a trumpet wounds you . . . I have trumpet-mouth.' This

'I made lifelong friends. In my letters home, I wrote, "I am blissfully happy," and I really meant it.'

– Benedict Cumberbatch

theory seems questionable, however, as none of the other great trumpet players (Louis Armstrong, Miles Davis, Chet Baker, Gonzo from *The Muppets*) have got Benedict-mouth . . . which must be a cause of deep sorrow to them all.

TOP HAT AND CANE

When Benedict was twelve, Wimothy bought a seventeenth-century crofter's cottage in the beautiful Gloucestershire countryside, near Swindon. The pre-teen B'batch didn't get to live in it much, however, as – with the help of funds from his grandmother, together with an art scholarship he'd won – he was bound for posh school proper: Hogwarts. I mean, Harrow.

The renowned Harrow School for boys is a boarding school situated in North-West London, in the town of – you guessed it – Harrow. Obviously Benedict is totally, absolutely its most famous alumnus, but other well-known

Contrary to popular belief, B'batch did not attend Hogwarts School of Wizardry and Witchcraft. Here he is with his classmates at Harrow.

Harrovians include Winston Churchill, writer Lord Byron (Benedict himself has been compared to Byron by *Sherlock* creator Steven Moffat: 'It's a bit of a blessing that one of the hottest young actors on the planet at the moment happens to look like Sherlock Holmes. He's got that imperious style and he's a bit Byronic'), Cecil Beaton (amongst other visual artists) and actors James and Edward Fox. Harrow is one of the four boys-only full-boarding schools in Britain (the others being Eton, Winchester and Radley), so the competition to gain a place is fierce, especially if, like Benedict, you need to win a scholarship to help pay the fees. All four schools look like castles (just like Hogwarts), dress their pupils in strange outfits (cf. Hogwarts) – and are known for being 'character building' (which sounds considerably less fun than learning magic).

Harrow is considered to be one of the best schools in the UK and, frankly, it better be, considering the £33,000-a-year price tag (that's modern-day prices, not Cumberprices) attached to a Harrovian education. In a BBC press release for the period drama *To the Ends of the Earth*, Benedict spoke of the class issues he encountered there. 'My grandmother paid for two thirds of my fee, so I was a very middle-class kid by most standards. I was surrounded by Lord Rothschild's son, Prince Hussein's son, dignitaries, princes and peers, left, right and centre.' (No doubt a good preparation for playing all those aristocratic roles later in life!)

Teenaged Benedict was kitted out in the regulatory Harrow uniform, which

'On Holmes, Martin kept saying, "Oh yeah, you went to fucking Hogwarts, didn't you?" And that's what my schooldays were like: Swallows and Amazons and Hogwarts. Martin is spot on that these schools are magical places if you know how to use them right.'

— *Benedict Cumberbatch*

is the same to this day (and will no doubt remain so for the next couple of millennia). It includes: morning suit, straw hat (aka 'boater') or top hat, depending on the season, and cane. Yes, that's right, a *cane*. (Whoever thought it would be a good idea to equip 800 boys aged 13-18 with canes must have had a very strange sense of humour indeed.) Recently, a Sky TV reality show went behind the scenes to uncover the truth about life at Harrow (*Harrow: A Very British School*), showing what it's like living in a boarding house with hundreds of teenage boys with canes. The impressive school theatre, complete with professional-standard props and costumes – and boys positively leaping at the chance to don a dress and play the girly roles – was heavily featured. If only the documentary had been made twenty-five years ago we could have seen Benedict bouncing across the stage

Every parent's nightmare, every girl's dream: Benedict stars as wannabe love machine Rory Slippery in TV series *Fortysomething*, 2003.

in a variety of guises, often female. He says, 'In my first year I had the fairly onerous task, having established myself as a reasonably decent rugby-playing cricketer and footballer, of starring as Titania, Queen of the Fairies [in Shakespeare's *A Midsummer Night's Dream*].' He then played Rosalind, the romantic female lead in Shakespeare's *As You Like It*, putting in a performance that his starry-eyed drama tutor called 'the finest since Vanessa Redgrave's'. Confusingly, Rosalind spends much of the play dressed as a man called Ganymede. So that made Benedict a man, playing a woman, playing a man. Which is, of course, exactly how it was done in Shakespeare's day when women weren't allowed on the stage. Trust Harrow to be as progressive as the seventeenth century.

Benedict was an integral part of the Rattigan Society, the school's main drama society, which is named after Sir Terence Rattigan, famous playwright and old Harrovian. Coincidentally,

'I felt confident about the world. Not … entitled. Just like … I could step into the world. Investigate it.'

– Benedict Cumberbatch

Benedict's first role at the National Theatre was in a Rattigan play, *After the Dance*, in 2010. The play is about bright young things being decadent and world-weary in the 1920s. At the time, speaking with the *Scotsman*, Benedict reminisced about being back in 'Ratt Soc' at Harrow: 'My first, big, silly role at school was as Arthur Crocker-Harris in Rattigan's *The Browning Version*, where my job was to make schoolmasters' wives weep with recognition.' Though the name of his character may have slipped his mind in this particular interview, (there's no 'Arthur' in *The Browning Version*; only 'Andrew'), Benedict was no doubt as brilliant playing Andrew Crocker-Harris at Harrow as he was as David Scott-Fowler at the National (*After the Dance* won four Olivier Awards and was declared by the *Times* to be the best theatrical production of 2010).

The school drama teacher in Benedict's day, Martin Tyrell, praised the young B'batch as, 'the best schoolboy actor [I] have ever worked with.' Well it wasn't gonna be Churchill, was it?

Maybe Harrow should consider a drama soc name change? 'The Cumberbatch Society' has a certain ring to it.

A MIDSUMMER NIGHT'S QUESTION MARK

We pause here in our linear analysis of the Cumberchildhood, to examine a mysterious issue, namely: when did the Benechild first appear in Shakespeare's *A Midsummer Night's Dream* and what part did he play? If you are experienced in the field of Cumberresearch you will no doubt have encountered conflicting evidence. Some sources suggest it was at Brambletye that Benedict first appeared in *Dream*, playing the role of Bottom, the hapless weaver and head of the Mechanicals, who at one stage has his head turned into that of a donkey. Another source claims it was at Harrow that Benedict first appeared in the play, in the role of Titania, Queen of the Fairies (who is bewitched to fall in love with the donkey-headed Bottom). However, the plot thickens as another source has him down as playing Helena, the tall skinny human girl (she's referred to as a 'maypole' at one point) who's unlucky in love. Tall and skinny . . . yes, that *does* sound like Benedict type-casting. Girl . . . less so. (But clearly as a kid he was the go-to guy for female roles . . . and I presume he wasn't quite 6'1/2" tall at that point either.)

So what came first for Benedict: Bottom, Titania or Helena? *How will we ever know?* Personally, I like to imagine that he played *all* these roles. In the same production. Or how about a one-man show in which Benedict gets to utilise his gifts for impersonation, transformation and cross-dressing to the full: *A Cumbersummer Night's Dream*. Theatre producers, take note.

Even so, it wouldn't be very scientific to leave this matter unresolved. Sherlock would most definitely not approve. So I can now officially put you out of your misery by revealing that, long before Harrow (well, a few months anyway), Benedict, aged twelve, did indeed play Bottom the Weaver at Brambletye. The year was 1989 and he received one of his first ever reviews. In the school magazine. It reads as follows: 'Benedict Cumberbatch's Bottom will be long remembered.' If only that reviewer could have known how true his smug word play would prove. (If you don't know what I'm talking about you clearly haven't visited the Tumblr page dedicated to 'Benedict's Cumberbum'.) The review was embraced by Wimothy – unaware of how many more Benedict

A Midsummer Night's Donkey: twelve-year-old Benedict in the guise of Bottom *circa* 1989. Part-boy, part-mule – 100 percent unforgettable.

reviews there'd be to come — and 'ah, we all remember Benedict's Bottom,' is a Cumberfamily in-joke to this day.

NOBODY PUTS BENEDICT IN A CORNER

While for many the rigours of boarding-school life — uniform inspections, sharing dormitories, lessons on Saturdays, not being allowed to leave the grounds without permission — would be a complete nightmare, Benedict loved his school days. 'I really did. Sports and outings . . . I made lifelong friends. In my letters home, I wrote, "I am blissfully happy," and I really meant it.' (The idea of any teenage boy using the word 'blissfully' in any context whatsoever after about 1928 seems too outlandish to be true. Which is, of course, precisely why we love Benedict.)

If you're worrying that his stick-like physique, 'trumpet-mouth' and hyperactivity might have made him an easy target for bullies, don't. Benedict says he wasn't victimised at all. 'I felt confident about the world. Not . . . entitled. Just like . . . I could step into the world. Investigate it.' Spoken like a true mini-Sherlock. Though there was that one time when a boy did try to bully him — 'He made me feel insecure and shy, and all I wanted was to be confident and happy' — and Benedict pinned him up against a wall . . . That

Benedict rocks some short 'n' spiky Cumberhair at London's Theatre Royal in April 2005.

probably sent out quite a clear message of DON'T RUMBLE WITH THIS CUMBERBATCH. Very Sherlock (though *he* would probably have pushed said bully out of a window). Benedict's sportiness was no doubt also a very good thing should any rugger-buggers have considered giving him grief. He loved sport and played on the rugby team. Presumably, given his physique, he was better at running and dodging than tackling, and no doubt all that early practice racing-sweatily-to-school came in handy.

By all accounts the young B'batch was popular. He realised early on that he could get people to like him if he made them laugh. This was a helpful skill when it came to monitoring the little kids at school. 'You could make younger kids go to bed and brush their teeth on time if you made them laugh.' (Shouldn't they have matrons and housemasters to do those things? Seems weird to pay over £30k in fees for your child to be set to work putting other children to bed. Though it would be lovely to be tucked in by Benedict, of course.)

DESPERATELY SEEKING FEMALES

There was one massive downside of being a Cumberboarder, however, and that was the lack of girls. Twelve or thirteen is generally the age when boys' attitude to girls starts to shift from 'hell no' to 'hell-*oo*' and Benedict was longing for some exposure to the opposite sex. His other concern was his late physical development. Now, in his late thirties but able to pass for much younger, he's probably grateful for his elfishly youthful looks – but it wasn't much fun looking like a child when he wanted to be a man. 'I was a kid until I was eighteen, really,' he says, no doubt thanking his lucky stars that he was a creative liar who could invent great stories of all the action he'd had during the summer holidays . . . when in reality he wasn't getting a whole lot of lovin'. 'I was a bit Hugh Grant around women,' remembers B'batch. '"Good gosh, er, do you mind if I, erm, touch, ah, it? Gosh, I feel funny now."' (Nowadays, of course, women beg to be touched by him wherever he goes. Ah, the irony.)

> **'I was a bit Hugh Grant around women. "Good gosh, er, do you mind if I, erm, touch, ah, it? Gosh, I feel funny now."'**
>
> *– Benedict Cumberbatch*

If it wasn't for this lack of physical confidence we might all have seen a whole lot more of Benedict a lot sooner than we did. The director Andrew Birkin came to Harrow to audition boys for his film version of Ian McEwan's novel *The Cement Garden* – yup, the one about incestuous siblings – and Benedict was asked to audition for the lead role of Jack. After considering the subject matter, however, he decided not to attend. 'I was really prudish at that age and thought, "Fuck it, I don't want to take my clothes off." I was terrified. I didn't want anyone seeing what I looked like.' So the role went to Andrew Robertson, the world had to wait for years to see Benedict in the buff, and Benedict himself had to wait until *Atonement* to appear in a McEwan dramatisation.

When not joking around on or off-stage, racing across the rugby pitch, or worrying about his lack of grown-up muscle tone, Benedict cultivated the same artistic talent which had helped him get into Harrow in the first place. He loved painting and drawing. Like drama, art was in his blood. Wanda herself spent a year at art school before deciding on an acting career and Benedict had clearly inherited her talent. He became Harrow's artist in residence and was given a wall in the school gym on which to express himself. (Bet Harrow wish they'd kept all that Cumberart – it would be worth almost as much as a pupil's termly school fees by now . . . almost.)

'Hello, I'm English.' Lighting up the red carpet with wonky grin plus wonky bowtie at the closing ceremony of 2004's Monte Carlo Television Festival, Monaco.

SHERLOCK SMARTS

Benedict is predictably modest about his intellectual achievements, claiming he was 'not that clever. Not ridiculously clever. Sharpish – I was a quick learner. A good impersonator.' Yup, the B'batch enjoyment of impersonations that we've come to know and love (you've seen him do his 'Alan-Rickman-in-the-guise-of-Severus-Snape' on *The Simpsons*, right? And his legendary 'Graham Norton'? If not, please hurry to YouTube and rectify this immediately) was one he used at Harrow. 'I used to mess around with Dictaphones at school and do interpretations and impersonations of people.' Whatever he says, Benedict was clearly pretty darn clever. And he had that whole geeky thirst-for-knowledge thing going on. When interviewed by Caitlin Moran in the *Times*, he described

> **'I've always been after the idea of betterment – to know exactly everything about that wine, and tell you about the birdsong I can hear, and to understand the world around me.'**
>
> *– Benedict Cumberbatch*

seeing the Harrow library for the first time (spoiler: he had Nerd Panic). 'I thought, I probably won't have a lifetime long enough to read the first shelf – let alone the first room, let alone the whole fucking library. I've always been after the idea of betterment – to know exactly everything about that wine, and tell you about the birdsong I can hear, and to understand the world around me.'

Unsurprisingly, Benedict did very well in his exams – surpassing his B.C. initials and scoring plenty of As at GSCE. His teachers predicted great things for his A-levels, and envisaged him going on to study at Oxford or Cambridge. But then something happened.

'POT AND GIRLS AND MUSIC'

In Benedict's last year at school, things changed. His body was finally developing into that toned mass of lean muscle we know and are strangely obsessed with. This bodily change coincided with top-year school privileges that allowed him access to the outside world, aka GIRLS. So he could at last properly discover the female of the species. And she could discover him. This turn up for the books caused Benedict to put down his actual books and go exploring. In his own words, this is when he was initiated into the intriguing world of 'pot and girls

An immaculately tanned Benedict graces the Los Angeles premiere of *Starter for 10* at the Arclight Theatre, February 2007.

and music'. I'm guessing at this point he got to use his 'trumpet mouth' for something other than music making . . .

During his last year at school, Benedict had another brush with death. It was the school holidays and he was in his bedroom studying for his A-levels. Suddenly a huge explosion shook the house. All the windows were shattered and he was engulfed in a massive dust cloud. Benedict had been a minor victim of the 1994 attack on the Israeli Embassy; a car packed with 30lbs of explosives had detonated. Luckily he and his parents were fine, though the blast did make B'batch temporarily deaf in one ear.

This near-disaster aside, the other distractions keeping Benedict from his schoolwork were generally more predictable: yup, it was girls, music and pot. Benedict's grades suffered, or, as he himself puts it, 'I got a bit lazy.' He didn't get the A-level results his teachers had hoped for. With Oxbridge no longer an option, he took a year out after leaving Harrow to consider his options. His parents wanted him to be a criminal barrister (he'd certainly have looked darn dashing in the white curly wig – he wears several as the Right Honourable William Pitt in harrowing slave drama, *Amazing Grace*, and totally rocks the style) but Benedict felt the pull of a thespian lifestyle.

Rather than make any rash decisions, he became a perfumier.

PERFUME

For six months, Benedict worked in a perfumier's, learning all about scents, high notes, base notes, essences and blends, i.e. what smells work together. This obviously leads to the question: why on earth wasn't Benedict cast as the lead in the film version of Patrick Süskind's novel, *Perfume*? It's the story of Jean-Baptiste Grenouille, a creepy French boy/monster-turned-murderer who trains as a perfumier because he has an eerily good sense of smell. The Cumbernose seems the absolutely most obvious and perfect choice for the role. Especially since the screenplay was written by Andrew Birkin, whom he'd already stood up at that *Cement Garden* audition. I can just see Benedict creepily stalking the back alleys of Paris, his hair matted with dirt, sniffing out virgin victims whose scent he can bottle. Ah well, couldawouldasmelledya. And Ben Whishaw, who ended up playing the role, did a good job too. I suppose.

ONE YEAR IN TIBET

Having made and saved some money from his sweet-scented job, Benedict headed to a Tibetan monastery in Darjeeling, India, to spend the remainder of his gap year teaching English to monks. Of course he did. While everyone else spent their 'gap yah' on a *Home and Away* bus tour of Australia, bungee jumping in Thailand or clubbing in Ibiza, Benedict was

'I could actually stay with monks in their home and watch them at work and at prayer, and get the chance to teach them and interact with them.'

– Benedict Cumberbatch

nurturing his inner chi. He explains the set up as follows: 'I could actually stay with monks in their home and watch them at work and at prayer, and get the chance to teach them and interact with them.' When asked what he learned from this he says, 'There's an ability to focus and have a real sort of purity of purpose and attention and not be too distracted. And to feel very alive to your environment, to know what you are part of, to understand what is going on in your peripheral vision and behind you, as well [as] what is in front of you. That definitely came from that.' To this day he considers himself a Buddhist, 'at least philosophically.'

During this year of exploration, Benedict nearly died (yes, again). He took a week out from the Tibetan Monastery and went on a trek around Nepal with four friends. Putting it mildly, they did not pay Sherlockian attention to detail when preparing for this holiday: none of them knew the area; they did not employ a guide; they did not wear appropriate clothing; and they did not bring supplies of food or water. The result was: lost in the Nepalese wilderness with nothing to

CUMBERSTATS

Name: Benedict Timothy Carlton Cumberbatch
DOB: Monday, 19 July 1976
Height: 6'1/2" (183cm)
Weight: Varies. (Muscle-to-skin-and-bone ratio is totes dependent on the requirements of each new role. Natch.)
Eye colour: Mixed. Like David Bowie, Benedict has the eye condition heterochromia, which means he has different-coloured eyes. Each of his irises has a different combination of gold, green and blue.
Natural hair colour: He calls it 'auburn'. (His way of saying 'a bit ginger'?)

eat or drink. As dehydration combined with altitude sickness started to send them all a little crazy, Benedict resorted to sucking moisture from a lump of moss. After nearly two days the group found their way to safety by following a trail of yak droppings. Benedict told *Event* magazine, 'We got altitude sickness and then amoebic dysentery. We were lost for a day and a half, trekking at night and squeezing moss to get water. We slept in an animal hut that stank of dung and had hallucinogenic dreams because of altitude sickness.' Thank god for the yak poo – without it Benedict might still be in that hut.

CHOICES

When he returned to London, skinny as ever, but somewhat more flexible thanks to regular yoga practice, it was time to take a deep *oooom*ing breath and make some big decisions. What should he devote his Cumberlife to? Should he choose a reliable 9-5 job, or risk the unpredictable life of a performer? His parents emphatically did not recommend acting as a career. They still thought he should be a lawyer or a . . . well, an anything that wasn't an actor really. They dreaded seeing their only son resign himself to a lifetime of uncertainty, rejection and unfairness. You can see their point: an acting career is a gamble with about as much chance of winning big as actual gambling. Maybe less. You can't blame

> '**You walk on stage – and you walk into a real world, for the people who are watching. It's amazing.**'
>
> *– Benedict Cumberbatch*

them for being cautious. I mean, they're English. So although *they* knew their Cumberspawn was exceptional, they were hardly going to be vulgar enough to suggest that he was born to win the jackpot of global stardom, were they? That would be totally *déclassé*.

Luckily for him and his parents – not to mention the world – Benedict didn't take Wimothy's advice. He knew he needed to become an actor. Maybe it was the Buddhist-monastery-soul-searching that had granted him the certainty to make like a young Padawan and follow his dreams. (B'batch is rumoured to be signed to the upcoming *Star Wars* films – directed by J.J. Abrams, who worked with him on *Star Trek Into Darkness* – so this Yoda reference is completely relevant. Benedict himself has said, 'I mean, there's a possibility, of course there is,

'Calm down, everyone!' Even back in the day, B'batch's stage presence was a force to be reckoned with.

and J.J. knows how much I would love to be a part of it, simply because, more than *Star Trek*, it really was something I grew up with.' Lightsabers crossed then, Cumberbitches . . .)

But the most compelling reason for him to enter the acting profession was that he wanted to have *fun*; and for Benedict, acting had always seemed like fun. He remembers being little and going to see his dad in a West End play. He stood backstage and desperately wanted to run into a scene; so much so that Wanda had to restrain him. 'What kid wouldn't?' Benedict says in defence of his diminutive self. 'Have you ever been backstage? All the sets, with the name of the production on the back, with weights on the bottom of them to hold them steady. And in the wings, you see all that. But then you walk on stage – and you walk into a real world, for the people who are watching it. It's amazing.'

THE COLLEGE YEARS

Rather than go straight into showbiz, or apply to drama school, Benedict decided not to abandon his academic education entirely. That way, if the acting didn't work out, he'd have a degree to fall back on. Admittedly a degree in drama isn't the most useful of back-up plans, but he could always use it to teach, um, drama . . . or he could apply to do a law conversion course after graduating. He was accepted at Manchester University in northern England and arrived on campus excited, skinny – and bendy from his yogic gap year. He was not in Harrow anymore. Manchester was like a different country, full of people from a variety of backgrounds. Benedict relished being away from what he terms the 'cashmere jumpers' of his school days. (Presumably he didn't miss the top hats either. Or the canes.) 'I wanted less exclusivity,' he told the *Telegraph*. 'I wanted more of life.'

Benedict had no problems fitting into his new environs – not to mention an exciting new social circle. 'I had a thoroughly healthy – and unhealthy – mix of friends.' He was no longer at boarding school, no longer in a monastery (Harrovian or Tibetan) – there was no curfew, no Saturday school, but plenty of girls. In 1999 he met Olivia Poulet (also destined to become an actor – today she's best known for her roles in political satires *The Thick of It* and *In the Loop*), and the two became a couple.

Olivia Chicken (to translate her name) and Benedict's relationship survived the tricky post-university period of adjustment that sees so many college sweethearts split up. The two remained very much together (and incredibly cute) until 2011, when they separated amicably. If evidence were

needed of Benedict's perfection, surely this twelve-year relationship, spanning uni and drama school, with a woman he is still good friends with, is conclusive proof? In 2013 Benedict told *Vogue*, 'I love her, I adore her, always will.' Olivia is one lucky Poulet.

An important milestone occurred when Timothy travelled to Manchester to see his son play baddy Salieri in a university production of Peter Shaffer's *Amadeus*, a play about the rivalry between two eighteenth-century composers: Antonio Salieri and the more famous Wolfgang Amadeus Mozart. Benedict's performance greatly affected Timothy, as Benedict explains: '[H]e looked me in the eye and grabbed me by the shoulders and said, "You're better now than I ever was or will be. I think you'll have a wonderful life and career as an actor, and I can't wait to be a part of watching it." And I pretty much burst into tears.' Little wonder, considering B'batch's admission that, 'one of the reasons I get up in the morning is to make [my parents] proud.'

At last, Benedict had Wimothy's parental blessing.

> '**I love her, I adore her, always will.**'
>
> *– Benedict Cumberbatch on Olivia Poulet*

Cumberchicken: B'batch and Olivia show their support for London's Almeida Theatre, at a fundraising party in March 2007.

'One of the reasons I get up in the morning is to make my parents proud.'

— Benedict Cumberbatch

BENEDICT

CUMBERKID STUFF

First kiss
'Underwater. Mary. I was eleven.
The wettest lips you could possibly kiss. I think that was definitely
my first kiss. Unless I'd kissed a boy at school in a fucking play ...'

First acting experience
(This is often erroneously cited as his appearance in *A Midsummer Night's
Dream*, but Benedict was actually a seasoned pro by then,
having played none other than Jesus's stepdad.)
'As a very bossy Joseph in the Nativity play at primary school.
Apparently I pushed Mary offstage because she was taking too long.'
(I'm assuming this isn't the Mary of the underwater kiss – though she may
have forgiven him for his youthful pushiness by the time
he was eleven. I mean, who wouldn't?)

Earliest memory
Looking up at 'a vision of sky'.

First word
Helicopter. 'They were the biggest things in the sky.'

Favourite scent
'Bright citruses – bergamot, vetiver.'

Embarrassing childhood memory
'When I was six, I got stung by a wasp in a Greek market.
A widow pulled down my pants, held me upside down
and rubbed an onion on my bum.'

Benedict *circa* 2005 – note the emergence
of those razortastic Cumbercheekbones
we know and love (and want to lick).

CUMBERBATCH

BENEDRAMA

'If I'd had fame early on, I'd have been able to abuse it in the way that a young man should.'

– Benedict Cumberbatch

L AMDA

After Benedict graduated from Manchester University he immediately applied for more training. This time it was drama school proper. After rounds of gruelling auditions (declaiming monologues; singing songs; pretending to be various animals in movement workshops; and several interviews in which he sincerely promised a lifelong commitment to touring children's theatre/unpaid fringe festival improv shows/other non-glamorous stuff that most actors' lives are chock-full of) Benedict took up a place at the prestigious London Academy of Music and Dramatic Art (LAMDA). His course was entitled the One Year Classical Acting Course

Just as he is Harrow's most lauded alumnus, so Benedict is obviously *totally* the most famous person ever to attend LAMDA. Other well-known graduates include: Giles from *Buffy the Vampire Slayer* (Anthony Head), Slughorn from *Harry Potter and the Half-Blood Prince* (Jim Broadbent), Samantha from *Sex and the City* (Kim Cattrall), and Finnick from *The Hunger Games: Catching Fire* (Sam Claflin). A pretty impressive acting crew, but obviously none is more impressive than Benedict. Little wonder then that an agent singled the B'batch out and offered to represent him after seeing a LAMDA showcase.

Thanks to the producers for this cuddlesome 2005 photo-shoot, introducing the world to the rising star of lavish period drama, *To the Ends of the Earth*. Great use of knitwear.

SWORD FIGHTS
AND CERTIFICATES

Drama school is all about immersing yourself in your craft and pushing yourself to extremes in the exploration of different acting styles. And then there are all the extra skills you're encouraged (or possibly forced) to acquire, including:

Historical dancing – bet Benedict looked fabulous in medieval-style tights and knee breeches.

Stage fighting – options include sabre, sword and dagger, broadsword and buckler, unarmed combat and *épée*. Fighting skills are assessed by a practical exam and certificates in stage combat are awarded, so it's possible to fail if you can't coordinate your moves properly (or if you chop someone's arm off – yup, these are real weapons!) As *Sherlock* has proved, Benedict is one stealthy fighter, so he no doubt sailed through.

Accent training – after weeks of practising with accent coaches, students are assessed in an exam and certificates are awarded in things like 'Standard American', 'Northern Irish', 'Manchester' and, of course, 'Received Pronunciation'. Given his impersonation prowess – and the fact that RP is the Official Accent of Harrow – it's fair to assume that this element of dramatic schooling would have been a walk in the park for Benedict.

'THE PLAY'S THE THING'

As an actor, Benedict's interest was always first and foremost in the text. As he told *Interview Magazine*, 'I was [. . .] brought up in a very traditional, text-heavy, educational environment, where reading and the word and the script – "The play's the thing" – was my schooling, as well as my training [. . .] I did classical theatre training.' Benedict has spoken repeatedly of the importance of this classical training and is a devoted patron of LAMDA's Act Now! campaign to raise money for the drama school to modernise and renew its premises (with the current ones falling apart, a move is most definitely on the cards). Funding a drama school could seem like a frivolous cause to back, but Benedict stresses the significance of his alma mater, saying, 'Should we

'I was brought up in a very traditional environment, where reading and the word and the script – "the play's the thing" – was my schooling, as well as my training.'

– *Benedict Cumberbatch*

CUMBERLOVES

Want to have a cultural life resembling Benedict's? Here's an eclectic mix of reading and watching material recommended by the man himself.

Reading – 'Nabokov, Dostoyevsky, Dickens, Paul Auster, William Boyd, Ian McEwan, Martin Amis, Julian Barnes, Nancy Mitford, A.S. Byatt, Beryl Bainbridge, Hilary Mantel, Andrea Levy.'

Movies – '*Badlands, Elephant, The Shining, Let the Right One In, Zoolander, Withnail and I, Brief Encounter, I am Love, Michael Clayton, The Prophet*, the *Bourne* trilogy and anything from Michael Winterbottom and Steve Soderbergh, Kubrick and Hitchcock.'

TV – '*The Wire, The Office, The West Wing, Mad Men* and *The Sopranos* – the typical clichés of great American HBO box-set drama.'

fail to seize this opportunity, London will lose a vital artistic resource that nourishes the global performing-arts industry, contributes to our economy and enriches our cultural life.' And he has a point; without LAMDA we might have no Cumberstar – and then our cultural lives would suck beyond belief.

CUMBERNAMES

Seldom has a name attracted so much attention as Benedict's. Love it or hate it, it definitely sticks in the mind. When *Metro* enquired as to the story behind his 'fantastic name', he revealed, 'There's a sort of debate about that. Cumberbatch could be Welsh for a small valley dweller. The "cum" in

Cumberbatch is hill. I need to look into it. Benedict means blessed. My parents liked the sound of the name and felt slightly blessed because they'd been trying for a child for a very long time.' In case you were wondering if there's any religious motivation behind this holy choice of name, B'batch goes on to say, 'I'm not Catholic, so it's not that. They liked the idea of Benedict and Ben – the fact that it can be contracted. I think Toby was their second choice.' *Toby* Cumberbatch? Nope, Wimothy made the correct choice. Bless them.

As long as there have been stars, there have been stage names. Some actors have no choice but to change their name because there's already another showbizzer registered under the same name, e.g. *Little Britain* actor David Walliams (born David Williams). Some want to escape their family heritage and any ensuing pressure or unfair advantage, e.g. Nicolas Cage (born Nicolas Kim Coppola, nephew to *Godfather* director Francis Ford Coppola). Some are assigned new names by their agents, in the hope that it'll make their new signings sound more memorable, e.g. Marilyn Monroe (real name Norma Jeane Mortenson). Others want to sound more glamorous, e.g. Cary Grant (real name Archibald Alexander Leach – hm, that's a bit of a Cumbername, isn't it?). Benedict, on the other hand, wanted to sound more ordinary. He worried that what he refers to as his 'fluffy old name' would hinder his career. So he signed with his agent using the stage name Ben Carlton. 'Carlton' had worked for his father, and his parents' advice was definitely not to go with Cumberbatch.

However, six months on, the roles still weren't streaming in for struggling actor Ben Carlton. He explains, 'Then one day, I told someone in the business what I was really called and they said, "That's great, that's something you can use to stand out. Why don't you use it?"' 'Because it sounds like a fart in a bath,' was Benedict's response, but

The selfie had not yet been invented. Benedict gets a little snap-happy on the red carpet at the Monte Carlo Television Festival, July 2004.

he agreed to give it a go, against the advice of Wimothy, who still worried it was too strange a name for an actor to have. But the gamble paid off. With a new agent and his bath-farty old name, Benedict's CV quickly started filling up.

BENEVISION

Back in the early 2000s, most UK drama-school graduates made their TV debut in one of three long-running shows: gritty ITV police soap *The Bill*, BBC hospital drama *Casualty* or ITV period police drama *Heartbeat*. Benedict went down the latter route and landed his first TV role in the year 2000, playing a weak-willed posh kid named Charles in an episode of *Heartbeat*.

'He is a one-off . . . It's easy for people to say, "Wow, you are the next Johnny Depp." Benedict was never going to be the next anybody. He was always going to be just who he is.'

– Rebecca Hall

By appearing in this series, Benedict was upholding a family tradition as both halves of Wimothy had already played roles in this British institution, which has guest-starred a whole host of familiar names, including Michelle Dockery from *Downton Abbey*, singer Charlotte Church, and even 007 himself, Daniel Craig.

It seems the producers of the show weren't worried that young Benedict had made too much of an impact, as in 2004 he appeared in *Heartbeat* again. This time around B'batch was playing an arrogant young man with a passion for shooting named Toby. By this time he was definitely a mildly recognisable face, having: investigated genetically modified crops (as journalist Jeremy in *Fields of Gold*); been jilted by a lesbian (as Freddy in the TV adaptation of Sarah Waters' *Tipping the Velvet* – 'I

Posing with his *Fortysomething* family in 2003. Is it weird that Benedict is staring at Duckface's boobs? Hugh Laurie doesn't seem too happy about it.

was the boy that turned a girlfriend into the most celebrated lesbian on television. I got so much stick for that' – I blame his terrible choice of baker-boy cap); fraternised with the spies who betrayed Britain (as Edward Hand in *Cambridge Spies*, alongside Tom Hollander, Toby Stephens, Samuel West and Rupert Penry-Jones); and played the sex-obsessed son of Hugh Laurie (Rory Slippery in comedy drama series *Fortysomething*). He also featured in a documentary about Dunkirk (the imaginatively titled, *Dunkirk*), and appeared in one-off episodes of two long-running crime series: *Silent Witness*, playing Warren, a forensic student with woman trouble (as so often with one-off guest-star appearances on crime shows, things don't end so well for Warren); and *Spooks,* playing Jim North, who leaks government information – practice for Benedict's later role as WikiLeaks mastermind Julian Assange, maybe?

BRUSHES WITH CUMBERDEATH

Benedict has defied death in real – as well as Sherlock – life. Here's how …

1. Hypothermia – Baby Benedict nearly froze to death on the roof, but was defrosted on a radiator. Phew!

2. Bomb – The 1994 attack on the Israeli Embassy in London caused all the windows in Benedict's family home to shatter. Luckily he escaped unscathed except for temporary deafness in one ear.

3. Dehydration and amoebic dysentery – On a trek in Nepal, Benedict and his friends got completely lost with no food or drink. After sucking moisture from moss to stay alive, they followed a trail of yak droppings to safety.

4. Hijacked and kidnapped – While filming in South Africa, Benedict and two friends were kidnapped and held at gunpoint. Luckily Benedict managed to persuade his captors that they didn't want a dead Englishman on their hands. He and the other hostages were finally released unharmed. When speaking of the terrifying event, Benedict says, 'It taught me that you come into this world as you leave it, on your own. It's made me want to live a life slightly less ordinary.'

SHAKESPEARE IN THE PARK

When asked if he prefers live theatre or screen acting, Benedict's reply is as follows: though he loves both equally, the immediacy of theatre has always appealed to him, 'where you give something and the response to what you've created is a communion between you and the dark that contains however many people. It's thrilling not having a reflection other than through the people you're communicating with.'

At the start of the millennium, alongside his work on the small screen, Benedict was busy working his way through a variety of reasonably big roles in theatre. His first stage appearance out of LAMDA was in 2001 when he acted in two Shakespeare plays at the Open Air Theatre in Regent's Park in London. He played Ferdinand the King, the scholarly lover-who-tries-not-to-be-a-lover in *Love's Labour's Lost*, and returned to his childhood favourite, *A Midsummer Night's Dream*, this time as Demetrius, one of the male human lovers (so no need for cross-dressing or donkey ears). Benedict's childhood love of the theatre hadn't diminished one bit. 'One interviewer asked me if I was worried about being trapped in the theatre. I said, "It's the best place to be". I know it sounds wanky, but as an actor, the more I do it the more I need to do it.'

The following summer he was back on stage in Regent's Park for yet more Shakespeare: *As You Like It* (not playing

Ever since B'batch started at LAMDA back in 2001, Benedict + Shakespeare = a totally Bardilicious pairing. Behold this batch of evidence featuring BC as (clockwise from top-left): a swashbuckling Demetrius in *A Midsummer Night's Dream*; the lip-smacking Orlando in *As You Like It*; would-be peacemaker Benvolio in *Romeo and Juliet*; and Ferdinand the (beige-wearing) King, in *Love's Labour's Lost*.

Rosalind this time, but her love interest Orlando) and *Romeo and Juliet* (playing Benvolio, Romeo's cousin and would-be peacemaker.) He also got his singing on in a production of epic musical *Oh, What a Lovely War!*

'It's thrilling not having a reflection other than through the people you're communicating with.'

– *Benedict Cumberbatch on the theatre*

'Texting and talking
have become a real
problem. But you have to
understand that you can't
demand an audience's
attention; you have
to command it.'
– Benedict Cumberbatch

Year of the Norse: in 2004 Benedict was positively
assailed with Scandinavian scripts. Here he is as
poor old Tesman in *Hedda Gabler* (above) and a
dashing Hans Lyngstrand in *The Lady from the Sea*
(below, good use of hat).

BENEDICT

GOING NORSE

In 2004 Benedict's stage work went all Norwegian when he appeared in the Almeida production of Henrik Ibsen's *The Lady from the Sea,* playing the young and naive Hans Lyngstrand. The following year he played Tesman, the try-hard academic husband of the tragic protagonist in Ibsen's *Hedda Gabler*, also staged at the Almeida. Winning rave reviews across the board, the production was such a success that it transferred to London's West End and Benedict was nominated for Best Supporting Actor at the 2006 Olivier Awards (he didn't win). But I'm getting ahead of myself. Let's rewind back to 2004, when Benedict scored his first major film role, playing the cleverest man in the world.

BEING HAWKING

The BBC film *Hawking* put Benedict firmly on the critics' map of Seriously Good Actors. As he himself puts it, 'Landing the role of Stephen Hawking was the most positively surprising thing that has happened to me.' The made-for-TV movie explores the student years of theoretical physicist and cosmologist Stephen Hawking, author of the groundbreaking *A Brief History of Time*. Benedict portrays Hawking as a twenty-one-year-old Cambridge student, struggling to find a topic for his PhD while coming to terms with his diagnosis of motor neurone disease – the illness which would eventually leave him paralysed and only able to speak through a computerised speech synthesiser. The role was a huge deal for Benedict; not only was it the biggest part he'd had to date, but he was playing someone real, someone who was alive and would be able to watch the film. And he would be portraying disability. 'I felt a huge onus of responsibility to get that part of his life right,' Benedict explains in a 2013 documentary about Stephen Hawking. 'It's a terrifying prospect to have a completely functioning mind inside a body that locks you in, that keeps you stationary.' He met with Hawking himself and experienced another moment of Nerd Panic. 'He's such a presence and you have to really know what you want to say to him or ask him because it takes such a huge, phenomenal effort for him to communicate with you. You think, "I really don't want to waste this man's time".'

Critics didn't think *Hawking* was a waste of anyone's time, and Benedict received glowing praise for his performance, as well as his first BAFTA nomination for Best Actor (he didn't win) and his first nomination for the Golden Nymph Best Actor Award at the Monte-Carlo TV Festival (he did win).

Though the niche film didn't attract a large audience, in the minds of the critics at least, the talent that is Benedict Cumberbatch had most definitely arrived.

CUMBERBATCH

ACTION!

'Lines are very difficult to learn.'

– Benedict Cumberbatch

KIDNAPPED AT THE ENDS OF THE EARTH *To the Ends of the Earth* is a BBC TV miniseries based on a trilogy of novels by William Golding (of *Lord of the Flies* fame). Benedict was cast as the lead: an arrogant young British aristocrat named Edmund Talbot, who chronicles his journey to New South Wales in the early 1800s. The director David Attwood describes Benedict as a bit of a godsend. 'We found Benedict Cumberbatch fairly early,' he recalls. 'We needed a very good actor, someone young enough to be believable as an aristocrat, an almost slightly dislikeable

Revving it up: A biking B'batch prepares to set engines racing in 2006. (Not sure that moustache is a winner though ...)

character who is an adolescent in terms of his views of the world, his upbringing. But we also needed someone who could hold the screen for four and half hours, in every scene. We needed someone with experience who was not only a very good actor, but also with terrific comic timing. Benedict was the ideal answer to that.'

Benedict sums up the gist of the story in typical Cumberstyle. 'It is a sort of rock'n'roll 1812 period drama about a young man's gap year. It's full of filth, dirt, discovery, sex, drugs, dancing, love, spiritual awakenings and massive sweeping changes!' (And, presumably, yak droppings?)

Thrilled to be partaking in a historical gap yah, Benedict headed to the film set in South Africa. Little did he know that the shoot was to be life-changing in a very frightening sense . . .

In a break from filming, Benedict drove to the coast for some scuba diving. On the way back to the hotel his vehicle suffered a punctured tyre in the KwaZulu region, just north of Durban. The situation worried him, 'It was cold, and it was dark. I felt rotten. We were wary because that's a notoriously dangerous place to drive. Then – poof – the front-right tyre blows. So we got the spare, but that meant getting all of our luggage out. We were like sitting ducks, adverts for – not prosperity necessarily, but materialism.' His fears came true as he and his travel companions (*Coronation Street* actress Denise Black and a South African friend) were set upon by a group of six men who tied them up, bundled them into a car and drove off. 'They were like: "Look down! Look down! Put your hands on your heads! Look at the floor,"' Benedict later told the press. 'They started frisking us and said "Where's your money? Where's your drugs?" – We had smoked a bit of weed – "Where are your weapons?" And at that point, this adrenaline of fight or flight just exploded in my body. I was like, "Oh fuck, we're fucked!"'

During this terrifying experience

> ## 'I was like, "Oh fuck, we're fucked!"'
>
> *– Benedict Cumberbatch*

Benedict truly believed his time was up, especially when he felt the barrel of a gun pressed against the back of his head. 'I was scared, really scared,' he said to *The Hollywood Reporter*. 'I said: "What are you going to do with us? Are you going to kill us?" I was really worried that I was going to get raped or molested or just tortured or toyed with in some way, some act of control and savagery.' The kidnappers tried to force him into the boot of the car, which is when his inner-Sherlock kicked in. Incredibly, he managed to talk them out of it using logic. 'I just tried to explain to them: "I will die, possibly have a fit, and it will be a problem for you. I will be a dead Englishman in your car. Not good."' His captors saw the sense in this and threw him back in the car with the others.

Finally they were driven into the middle of nowhere. 'We were hauled out and told to kneel with our hands on our heads. We were in the execution position with a duvet over our heads to silence the shots. . . they took me up to a small hill away from the others and tied my hands behind my back with laces from the trainers they'd removed earlier.' The others were brought up the hill and forced down beside B'batch. After three hours shivering in the cold on the hillside, the victims ran for help and called the police. 'I kind of thank God I had the presence of mind to give them the idea that it would be better to keep me alive. And the other two hadn't been harmed,' says Benedict. 'I've still got a scar where I was tied up. It was terrifying. The next morning I woke up as a free man with the sun on my face and I cried. I thought I'd never feel its warmth again.' Poor B'batch, that's one heck of a shiversome experience; but on the plus side I reckon the Cumberscar (on his inner wrist, fyi) gives him major wounded-hero appeal!

Despite this traumatic event, the miniseries was completed and was another hit with the critics. It also earned Benedict his second Golden Nymph Award for Best Actor. But I reckon coming home alive was the bigger reward – even if Olivia wasn't there at the airport, awaiting him with open arms . . .

Yep, that's right. Benedict totally knows the pain of being dumped by the person you always believed to be The One. In fact, Olivia chickened out of the relationship before he even left for the South African shoot. He arrived on location dazed, confused and still reeling from the bombshell that they were over. 'My break-up was completely out of the blue,' he revealed in interview with the BBC Press department. 'I had been very nervous for us because of where we were in our relationship and because I was going away for such a long time.

'I say, can I skydive in this?' Resplendent in cravat, waistcoat and tails, B'batch looks regal as arrogant aristo Edmund Talbot in 2004's *To the Ends of the Earth*. The South African shoot proved exhilarating in more ways than one . . .

It was a cause for anxiety, but the actual break-up itself was a big surprise. That heartbroken feeling was painful and I thought, "I have to be resourceful". I was so buoyed up by the people around me in South Africa – they were family.' (Well, except for the kidnappers . . .)

Is that a helicopter? No, it's Benedict and he can fly! Well, he can fall through the sky. Here he takes the plunge in Queenstown, New Zealand. The man fortunate enough to be strapped to his cumberback is instructor Mauricio Rochas.

B'batch's Cumberheart must have healed quicker than most, however. In later interviews, he barely even refers to this blip in the couple's timeline, citing the Olivia Years as spanning 1999 – 2011 . . . so clearly post-South-Africa Benedict's Cumbercharms won her back before too long. (I bet the whole wounded-hero scar thing helped . . .)

WIGGING OUT

In 2008 the *Guardian* reported that the name 'Cumberbatch' can be traced back to Germany (er, what happened to Wales?) and that Benedict's ancestors were prominent slave traders in the Caribbean. According to this piece, '[Benedict] says, half-jokingly, that his role as William Pitt in the abolitionist

FIRSTS AT THE ENDS OF THE EARTH

Aside from the kidnap, filming To the Ends of the Earth *provided a number of other firsts for Benedict.*

First sex scene. (With on-screen love interest Zenobia, played by Paula Jennings). At the time Benedict said, 'My on-screen sex technique is not perfected but I hope it worked! Edmund [...] behaves with Zenobia like a sexual animal: he's very avaricious and knowing. He's charming and flirts with her from the first day he sees her and he goes straight for the kill.'

First scuba dive. 'I learnt to scuba dive in one of the most beautiful places on God's earth, about a three-hour drive from where we were filming.'

First swim with whales. 'On my second dive I swam with a whale, who was about ten feet away from me. It was magical, the most beautiful sight and it had a baby whale swimming by its head.'

First swim with sharks. 'I went swimming with great white sharks. I was in a cage and they were fed just beside us. It was terrifying and wonderful – they are such a potent force of nature.'

First sky dive. 'I did a really touristy thing and I got a video made of my jump. There is an unflattering film of me, double chin flapping around my ears, going through the G-Force and going "oh-my-God" and a lot worse! [...] It was the most exquisite sensation and when I landed on the ground I wanted to do it again. I felt incredibly horny as well, because it's such an extreme thing. You think, "God, I've just had the most massive bite out of life and I'm really hungry for more".'

'There is an unflattering film of me, double chin flapping around my ears, going through the G-Force and going "oh-my-God" – and a lot worse!'

– Benedict Cumberbatch on skydiving

sporting a variety of strange, curly (and sometimes powdered) wigs.

To prepare for the role, Benedict asked to be shown around the House of Commons by Pitt's biographer, the then shadow foreign secretary, William Hague. The research paid off; though the Anglo-American film features an impressive cast, including Albert Finney, Michael Gambon, Romola Garai and singer Youssou N'Dour, it was Benedict who secured the film's only acting-award nomination, the London Critics Circle Film Award for Breakthrough in Acting (he didn't win).

ANNOYING JAMES MCAVOY, PART I

At this point in his career, Benedict began landing the part of 'guy who bugs James McAvoy'. In the 2006 comedy *Starter for 10*, based on the novel by David Nicholls (author of bestseller *One Day*), he plays the posh, ginger-haired, quiz-obsessed post-grad student Patrick Watts, who has built his life around the dream of winning the legendary BBC television quiz, *University Challenge*. Essex new boy Brian – a floppy-haired James McAvoy – gets on Patrick's nerves by threatening his position as General Knowledge God. Patrick therefore sets out to make Brian's life on the quiz team as difficult as possible. Set in Thatcher's Britain of 1985 and starring a crew of young Brit actors, many of whom have gone

'Does my head look weird in this?' Back in period garb for 2006's *Amazing Graze*, Benedict – in the guise of William Pitt the Younger – enjoys one of several strange wigs.

film *Amazing Grace* was a sort of apology [for his slave-trading forebears].'

Released in 2006, *Amazing Grace* tells the story of Britain's route to abandoning the slave trade in the late 1700s. Ioan Gruffudd stars as William Wilberforce, campaigner for the abolition of slavery, while Benedict plays William Pitt the Younger, the Prime Minister of the day, abolitionist and friend of Wilberforce,

on to become Hollywood stars (not just Benedict and James McAvoy, but Rebecca Hall, Alice Eve and James Corden, no less), this very British film was – somewhat bizarrely – produced by Tom Hanks.

Despite this melding of super-stardom it was not a global success, with Hanks blaming this on the intrinsic Britishness of the references to *University Challenge* and its then host, Bamber Gascoigne (played in the movie by none other than *Sherlock* co-creator and Mycroft himself, Mark

Universally challenged: A black-eyed Benedict with the *Starter for 10* cast in 2006. From left to right: Alice Eve, James McAvoy, Mark Gatiss, B'batch himself and Elaine Tan.

Gatiss). In a *Radio Times* interview Hanks explained, 'You know, in America they wanted to call it *Brian Knows Everything*?' because the iconic phrase 'Starter for 10' (which heralds each new starter question on *University Challenge*) is meaningless to non-British audiences. But even those *au fait* with all the rules of *UC* didn't necessarily enjoy the film; several critics found it a

Putting the 'cad' in Cadbury. Juno Temple's Lola prepares to wed uber-creepy chocolatier Paul Marshall in 2007's *Atonement*.

tad banal. Peter Bradshaw commented in the *Guardian,* 'Much of the love story and the comedy is formulaic, offering only a romanticised version of the embarrassments and horror of going to college for the first time.' Once again, however, Benedict's frenzied and hilarious performance was pretty much universally praised. From the moment he first barks, 'Haaalt!' at a confused Jimmy Macca, he steals the show, managing to make some pretty predictable scenes very watchable.

ANNOYING JAMES MCAVOY, PART II

The next B'batch-Macca face-off occurred the following year, in 2007's

Bros before roles: Benedict and James McAvoy attend the *Starter for 10* premiere at the Notting Hill Arts Club in London, November 2006.

Atonement. The dramatisation of Ian McEwan's award-winning novel features James McAvoy as the unfortunate Robbie Turner, who is accused of a crime he never committed. Sporting a particularly sinister moustache, Benedict played his creepiest role to date, Paul Marshall, slimy sleaze ball and – SPOILER ALERT – actual criminal of the story. Once again, James and Benedict were cast on opposite sides of the class divide; Robbie is the son of a housekeeper whose employees have paid for his Cambridge University education, whereas Paul, also Cambridge-educated, is a rich chocolate-factory owner destined to become a Lord. Benedict's breathy admonition to the teenage Lola (played by Juno Temple), as he hands her a chocolate bar, to 'bite it; you have to *bite it,*' is delightfully disturbing. Shudder. He makes Willy Wonka seem like babysitter of the year.

THE OTHER BOLEYN BOY

Though the trailer for period movie *The Other Boleyn Girl* suggests that the only man of the film is Eric Bana (playing a pre-obesity Henry VIII), the movie itself does feature a smattering of Benedict. He plays the complicit cuckold William Carey, husband of Mary Boleyn (Scarlett Johansson), who

thinks that letting his wife sleep with the King is a pretty spiffing idea, don'tcha know, as it might lead to a frightfully nice castle. Unsurprisingly, things don't work out quite as planned.

Benedict shows his range in this heavily-fictionalised reworking of history (based on the novel by Philippa Gregory), managing to be totally convincing as the gormless William. And he wears the knee-britches, lace collars and a charmingly vile pancake hat with assurance. Tudor-licious!

Smocking hot. Looking Tudor-licious as cuckolded husband William Carey in *The Other Boleyn Girl*, 2008.

CUMBER-LOOK-A-LIKES

*Top five things fans think
Benedict looks like:*

1. An otter
2. A glass of milk
3. A hammerhead shark
4. White asparagus
5. Sid the sloth from the
   Ice Age movies

GAGA FOR RADIO

Benedict has always enjoyed radio acting. Before going to drama school, when imagining an acting career, he prophetically envisioned: 'theatre first, then a bit of telly, and then possibly film – if you're lucky. And hopefully some radio work to use the pipes in that medium because I do love radio.' And he really does – not just appearing on it, but listening to it, as he told the *Radio Times*, 'I love Radio 3. I'm Radio 3 in the car as well. And Radio 4: I change between the two; I'm not religious about it. Radio's something I go back to if I've been out of the country for any length of time. I still find the magical art [when acting on radio] of what effect you are having, how the space is constructed, what the mic's doing, is a mystery. It's nice to really intensely concentrate on and listen to the word and the sense of the word. Radio's a joy. It's just a joy.'

'It's nice to really intensely concentrate on and listen to the word and the sense of the word. Radio's a joy. It's just a joy.'

– Benedict Cumberbatch

His voice first graced the airwaves playing Captain Nigel Rowan in BBC Radio 4's 2004 adaptation of Paul Scott's *The Raj Quartet*. Over the years his Cumbertones have featured in many other radio dramas, notably in the recurring role of Young Rumpole to (LAMDA President) Timothy West's Older Rumpole in seven adaptations of John Mortimer's novels about the ageing barrister.

In 2013 he played the Angel Islington in Neil Gaiman's *Neverwhere*, which saw Benedict re-uniting with old pal James McAvoy, who plays the lead character, Richard Mayhew. One day there will surely be a production in which Benedict has the lead and James plays a supporting role. Surely?

BROODYBATCH

Over the years, Benedict has made no secret of the fact that he'd simply love to settle down and start a family . . . with the right woman, of course. In 2010 he told the *Telegraph*, 'I am very broody.' Apparently this longing for fatherhood struck Benedict in his late twenties and is by no means an attempt to be progressive and metrosexual trendy. 'I have been broody for the last five years because I have two godchildren and Olivia has got nephews, too. I am not racingly modern; that is just where my head is at the moment.' He went on to say that he would like children before he turned thirty-five. That didn't happen. And in a 2013 interview with *ELLE*

'I'm at the age now where I can play dads, so it's a new thing to put myself into that headspace . . . then again, I think it's something that always takes you by surprise. When are you ever settled enough to have kids?'

– *Benedict Cumberbatch*

Japan Benedict seemed calmer about the parental urge. 'It is a wonderful thing to get married young and become a father. I used to think that I'd get married in my mid-thirties and have children. But now I think I can wait. I'm no longer in a hurry to get married.'

Benedict doesn't see himself as the type for whirlwind romances and shotgun weddings. He shattered the hearts of millions of fans hoping he'd catch their eye amid a crowd of screaming Cumberbitches and spontaneously propose, when he declared, with Sherlockian rationality, 'I would like to first get to know the partner and build a trusting relationship before making the commitment.' Fair enough. And he didn't say that partner couldn't be someone he'd met in a crowd of fans . . .

WORKING UP A STORM

Between 2009 and '10, Benedict appeared in an eclectic mix of films. In 2009's *Creation*, he played famous botanist Joseph Dalton Hooker, friend to Paul Bettany's Charles Darwin. The film explores Darwin's relationship with his family, as well as his struggles in writing his seminal work *On the Origin of Species*. Critics were generally positive about the film, though none appear to have commented on the fact that Benedict's luscious ginger-tinged locks, with matching stubble, contrast very effectively with Bettany's receding hairline.

DESPERATELY SEEKING MRS C . . .

*Ever wondered what the most perfect man
on the planet is seeking in a woman?
How you can become an irresistible Irene Adler to Benedict's smitten
Sherlock? Well, stop wondering and start researching. Contained within this
cunning fact box, you'll find each of Benedict's requirements for romance –
as told by the man himself.*

1. **Make him laugh.** 'I believe the sense of humour is important.'
2. **Be comfortable in your own skin.** 'A woman who knows that
she doesn't have to get all decked out to look good is sexy.'
3. **Be a bantering beauty.** 'A woman who can make you feel
smart with her conversation skills is also sexy.'
4. **Get behind team Benedict!** 'I also think someone who is good
at working with others is sexy. It's like playing a tennis doubles match.
You need to be able to work well together if you are
to stay as partners for a long time.'

**Women he admires (aside from his mother – aw – and his ex-
girlfriends – double aw):** Rebecca Hall, Keira Knightley, Meryl Streep.

**Benedict's dream date – follow this and he's guaranteed to Reichenbach
Fall for you:** 'Fantastic meal, no washing up! Great conversation,
time and enough laughter to get the digestion going.'

Benedict's dating disaster: 'One nightmare date with my ex was when
I became violently ill on the penultimate dinner of a gastro holiday in
Cornwall. The most expensive meal, which had been kept for last,
was ruined.' Hmm, yes, beware of violent laughter.
You don't want to 'get the digestion going' too thoroughly . . .

Benedict's simple but irresistible recipe for romance:
'a really lovely, super fruit and chicken salad.'

On the road to a breakthrough in 2009's *Creation*. From left to right: Toby Jones, Paul Bettany (as a balding Darwin) and B'batch (as well-thatched botanist Joseph Hooker).

Benedict embraced a family tradition by appearing in a classic crime adaptation in 2009. Timothy has featured in *Poirot* and *Midsomer Murders*, while Wanda's been in *Inspector Lewis* and *Hetty Wainthropp Investigates*; but neither of them had starred in a *Miss Marple* adaptation. So Benedict took that upon himself, playing Luke Fitzwilliam in Agatha Christie's *Murder Is Easy*. The TV movie stars Julia McKenzie as super-sleuth Jane Marple and features a cast heavy with British stars, including Anna Chancellor (who played Benedict's mother in *Fortysomething*, but is perhaps best known as Duckface in *Four Weddings and a Funeral*).

In 2010 Benedict appeared on the big screen in controversial dark comedy *Four Lions*, written and directed by Chris Morris of *Brass Eye* fame. The movie, which follows a group of hapless would-be suicide bombers, won several awards (including a BAFTA) and rave reviews, but failed to get distribution in many countries (including the USA), because of its subject matter. Benedict has a cameo as an inept hostage negotiator. When asked why he chose to be a part of the film, even though the role is small, he said that it was the chance to work with Chris Morris again (Benedict had appeared in two episodes

To die for: B'batch is tweedsomely gorgeous as Luke Fitzwilliam – the upstanding young detective who teams up with Miss Marple in TV mystery *Murder Is Easy*.

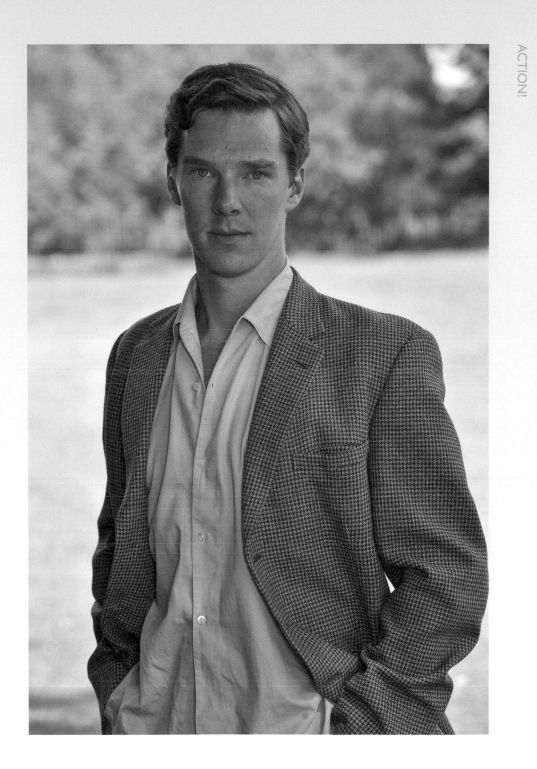

'I struggle to learn by rote. I've had meltdowns on set. Which is embarrassing and shameful.'

– Benedict Cumberbatch

of Morris's comedy show *Nathan Barley* back in 2005) that enticed him. 'I did *Nathan Barley*. I had drunk blokes coming up to me in the street all the time going, "You're the fucking Barley man!" No one comes up to me saying "You're Stephen Hawking!" None of that. Chris Morris is just extraordinary. He's very fucking gentlemanly, incredibly smart and quicksilver-witted. He said, "It's a really small part, mate," but I said, "I don't care." I'd sweep the fucking floor for him.' (Business idea: Cumbercleaning Services Ltd?)

Next it was back to biopic territory for Benedict. He took on the role of tormented artistic genius Vincent Van Gogh (of ear mutilation fame), in *Van Gogh: Painted with Words*, a BBC drama-documentary based on the letters Van Gogh wrote to his brother Theo. As a documentary about the arts, it was only seen by a very niche audience, but Benedict's performance was well-received by critics and the film won a Rockie for Best Arts Documentary at the Banff World Media Festival in 2011.

Tightly wound: Benedict's favourite stripes get another outing at the *Creation* premiere, held at London's Curzon cinema in September 2009. Who isn't jealous of that scarf?

The role of James in 2010 Brit flick *Third Star* is one of Benedict's little known starring roles. Twenty-nine-year-old James is in the late stages of cancer. He goes on holiday with a group of old friends to Wales, knowing this will be his last trip. In order to look close to death, Benedict (bizarrely) went on a healthy diet. 'I ate healthily, but there was no snacking, no drinking, no bread, no sugar, no smoking. Afterwards I had a pork belly roast.'

Though far from a critical or commercial success, this gently amusing but predictable bromance does have the merit of featuring Benedict in yet another variety of hat (check it out! His fetching fedora makes this movie well worth a look).

2010 seems to be the year for obscure Cumberbatch movies; anyone see *The Whistleblower*? It was inspired by the true life story of Kathryn Bolkovac, a US police officer who fought to expose a sex-trafficking ring while working as a peacekeeper in post-war Bosnia. Rachel Weisz plays Kathryn, while Benedict takes the role of Nick Kaufman, her peacekeeping superior, in possibly his most unpleasant part ever. Yes, even slimier than Paul 'Evil-Willy-Wonka' Marshall. Double shudder.

CUMBERTHATCH

'Pull the hair on my head the wrong way, and I would be on my knees begging for mercy. I have very sensitive follicles.'
– Benedict Cumberbatch

Obviously all actors undergo physical transformations for various roles during the course of their careers, but no one and no thing has ever been more chameleonic than that batch of wild keratin perched atop the Cumberhead. Those of you who first noticed him in *Sherlock* may assume that those waves are naturally dark, but that would be a false deduction. In an interview with *Esquire* magazine in 2010 Benedict outed himself as a bit of a ginger. Though he calls it 'auburn'. Either way, Benedict goes on to state emphatically, 'that's just not right for Sherlock. He's a creature of the night. He's got a dark, sociopathic side to him. The archetypal image of him is that he's a slick-looking, dark-haired gentleman.' Is society really not ready for an 'auburn' Holmes? Have we not come further than: dark hair equals creature of the night? Oh well, Benedict looks great as a brunette so whatevs.

Here's a brief guide to the rainbow that is Benedict's hair.

Sherlock dark. Because creatures of the night don't have red hair.

Bald, as the Monster in *Frankenstein*. (Is that a Mohawk or pus?)

BENEDICT

Dirty-blonde and unctuous for *Atonement.* (SPOILER ALERT! You can certainly judge this character by his unsavoury-looking 'tache.)

Ginger-nutty and side-parted in *Starter for 10.* It must have taken a few tonnes of Wella to eradicate those curls; you can see them trying to spring up every now and then (probably jealous of Bamber-Gascoigne-aka-Mark-Gatiss's grey 'fro).

Sandy blonde with The Biggest Fringe ever in *Tinker Tailor Soldier Spy.* (I think the mistake was taking straightening irons to the fringe …)

Assange-albino for *The Fifth Estate.* Hey, Benedict! Barbie called – she wants her peroxide back (and I think her call was being monitored by the government).

CUMBERBATCH

CUMBERFAME

'You can't imagine fame. You can only ever see it as an outsider and comment on it with the rueful wisdom of a non-participant.'

– Benedict Cumberbatch

DOCTOR NO Benedict seemed like an obvious choice to step into the Tardis when David Tennant's time as *Doctor Who* came to an end in 2010. B'batch was an up-and-coming name in UK television, admired by critics, directors and producers alike – and he had the kind of razor-sharp cheekbones that befit an alien Timelord (and look great on merchandising and action-toy figurines). *Doctor Who* creator Steven Moffat was very keen to get Cumberbatch on board. It all seemed perfect. But, although most actors would eat their own spleen to be part of a brand – branding equals fame plus big monies – Benedict is not most actors. Having discussed the matter with Tennant, he said no to *Doctor Who*, explaining, 'David and I talked about it, but I thought it would have to be radically different. And anyway, I didn't really like the whole package – being on school lunchboxes.' So Matt Smith became the new Timelord (and face of countless lunchboxes), leaving Benedict free to dive into another of Moffat's projects . . .

BIRTHING SHERLOCK

As writers of *Doctor Who*, Steven Moffat and Mark Gatiss had plenty of time to hang out together and soon discovered

'I play the man with the ironed fringe': when *Tinker Tailor Soldier Spy* opened the 2011 Ghent Film Festival, Benedict was there to represent. Natch.

Always in fashion: Matt Smith, aka Dr Who, and Benedict living it up at the *Esquire* and Tommy Hilfiger party, London, 2013.

'They're so gripping, really interesting, well thought-out, beautifully-drawn characters and a fantastic insight into playing very extraordinary people.'

– Benedict Cumberbatch

easy ways into this as an idea, and to explain to other people, is that in the very first, original story, Doctor Watson is invalided home from Afghanistan. And it's the same unwinnable war, virtually. Once you start thinking like that, the whole show makes total sense.' Moffat adds, 'There's very, very little you have to change at all to put Sherlock Holmes in the modern day.'

They knew that their version of the famous sleuth was going to have to be exceptional to stand out from the crowd of Holmses that have graced TV and cinema screens over the years, from Mack Sennett's performance in the 1911 film *The $500 Reward*, via famous names like Basil Rathbone (for many, the original and best . . . until Benedict came along), Christopher Lee (he's also played Sherlock's know-it-all bro Mycroft), John Cleese (twice!), Roger Moore (who recently replied to a complimentary tweet from Mark Gatiss, praising Moore's performance in *The*

that they shared a mutual love of Arthur Conan Doyle's work. They became obsessed with the idea of bringing the greatest of all detectives, Sherlock Holmes, to modern-day London, convinced it would work brilliantly. As Gatiss puts it, 'One of the wonderful,

Benedict's glossy blond fringe gets another outing at the American Express Gala screening of *The King's Speech* at the BFI London Film Festival, 2010.

Man Who Haunted Himself, 'Thank you. I might be equally wonderful in *Doctor Who* or *Sherlock* if asked' – cameo alert!), Christopher Plummer (James Mason was his Watson), Tom Baker (right after he'd played Doctor Who – are these two characters permanently linked?), Jeremy Brett (who played Holmes for ten years and then descended into mental illness), James D'Arcy (Benedict's fellow LAMDA alumnus), Rupert Everett (for the BBC in 2004) and Jonathan Pryce (for the BBC in 2007), to Robert Downey, Jr in 2009's Hollywood action blockbuster *Sherlock Holmes*, directed by Guy Ritchie. This adaptation sees Downey, Jr romping through a fog-filled

period London, administering punches and one-liners at crazed speed, with a buttoned-up Jude Law Watsoning at his side. When *Den of Geek* asked Moffat for his opinion on Ritchie's movie, he said, 'I think Robert Downey, Jr's done a great job of being Sherlock Holmes, but I'm never, ever going to look at him and believe he actually is Sherlock Holmes. He's too little, and he doesn't look like him. And his accent is shite!' (Hmm . . . so not *that* great a job of being Sherlock Holmes, then?)

One mission that MoffGat shared with Guy Ritchie was to reinforce the humorous aspect of Conan Doyle's original writing. Unlike Ritchie, however, they didn't want to get bogged down in recreating period detail – hansom cabs

Modern, dark, 'impish' and in it for da lolz: Benedict shows his perfect Sherlockian credentials, 2009.

and ornate opium pipes – they wanted to focus on the *fun* of the stories. Moffat said, 'Some of the Sherlock Holmes adaptations, they're treating it like it's Jane Austen or something, and they make it really boring and slow. And it's not. Sherlock Holmes isn't like that. It's something children would read.' MoffGat use the comparison of James Bond; no one expects the latest Bond adaptation to be set in the period the book was written in, so why shouldn't Holmes receive the same updating?

One thing the creators were keen to capture from Conan Doyle's original was the laughter. Moffat explains, 'Sherlock Holmes laughs all the time in the stories, he's always bursting out laughing, or roaring with laughter, or having a laugh. And Sherlock and Watson in the stories actually laugh together a lot. You never see it! He's always stern. He's not like that at all, he's quite impish.' Hmm, 'impish', remind you of any-Cumber-body?

BECOMING SHERLOCK

When Benedict first heard that Conan Doyle's famous deerstalkered detective was to be given a modern makeover, he didn't jump for joy and reach for the nearest trench coat and magnifying glass. No, he behaved in a far more Sherlockian way: he was deeply sceptical and rather dismissive, 'I thought, why fix something that ain't broke? I was very dubious about how cute it would be and what the purpose of using him was. Launch a franchise, get viewing figures, make money.' While the idea of being a franchise may be very attractive to most actors (remember, branding equals big monies), we know that Benedict had never hankered after being *Doctor-Who*-famous. However, he had always respected the work of Steven Moffat and Mark Gatiss, so when he heard that they were the team behind *Sherlock* he began to get excited. 'I then read the script [. . .] and I was blown away by it.' He felt sure MoffGat would want to stay true to Conan

Forget Neo from *The Matrix*; *this* is how to rock a long black trench. B'batch in Belstaff, filming *Sherlock* in Swansea, January 2009.

'I read the script . . . and I was blown away by it. It was so funny and so fast-paced and at the heart of it was just this incredible relationship with Watson. A wonderful friendship.'

– Benedict Cumberbatch

Doyle's original stories and he wasn't disappointed, '[the script] was so funny, and so fast-paced and at the heart of it was just this incredible relationship with Watson. A wonderful friendship.' Aw, Benedict agreed to be franchised for friendship – that's a truly heart-warming purse lining.

THE AUDITION

The Sherlock of *Sherlock* needed to be fiercely intelligent, striking, interesting and, of course, impish. Clearly there was only ever going to be one choice: B'batch. He was the only actor asked to audition for the role of Sherlock. That's how convinced Moffat and Gatiss were that he'd be perfect. Moffat loved his creepy performance in *Atonement* (shudder), and Gatiss could vouch for him professionally, having acted opposite him in *Starter for 10*.

Benedict recalls going to the legendary Beryl Vertue's flat in Holland

Doctor Who or Doctor No? B'batch arrives at the Prince's Trust Rock Gala, in November 2011, London – possibly paying homage to a Tom-Baker era Timelord.

Park for a reading (Ms Vertue is the unofficial queen of British television. She is also Moffat's mother-in-law and the executive producer of *Sherlock*. Her daughter Sue – Moffat's wife – is the show's producer. Guys, it's 'family', not nepotism . . .). B'batch describes the flat as 'a very grand version of Baker Street [with Beryl] serving the tea and biscuits, and it was a little bit like Mrs Hudson!' He gave the reading his all and was enthused by Moffat and Gatiss's dedication to their vision; he explains, 'I could see they both had total faith in the idea of it.'

Sherlock had found its Sherlock.

WHICH WATSON?

Every man's everyman (and every hobbit's everyhobbit) Martin Freeman is to Benedict as salt is to pepper, as Robin is to Batman, as Watson is to Holmes, in fact: an obvious pairing. And yet we nearly had a very different equation, because Matt Smith was the first actor to audition for the part of Doctor John Watson. Smith says, 'Well, I thought my audition for Watson was very good. But clearly not good enough! Basically they looked at it and went, "He's not Watson. It'd be like having two Sherlocks in the room." But Martin Freeman was born to play that part. And rightly so, thank the stars. I wasn't destined for Watson – but I met Steven Moffat, who said: "He'd be quite a good Doctor Who . . .""

Can you imagine the unholy clash of cheekbones had Matt Smith been Benedict's Watson? Sherlock and the good doctor would have sliced each other's faces every time they embraced in one of those manly displays of fraternal best-friendship. Thank God for apple-cheeked Marty F.

But Freeman was far from a shoo-in for the part. After his audition, MoffGat were convinced he wasn't interested in the role as he'd come across as grumpy and distracted. This was nothing to do with the part, however; it was actually down to some pesky thief stealing his wallet on his way to the audition. Freeman admitted to the *Radio Times*, 'I wasn't in the best frame of mind . . . maybe I was a bit stressed. But a week later my agent rang and said, "Listen, this *Sherlock* thing, they're sort of under the impression you weren't that into it."' Freeman hastened to put them straight by going back for a second audition. An all-round Sherson-Watlock love-in ensued. 'So I came in again, read with Benedict and it instantly worked [. . .] I thought he was a fantastic actor and

there was something about our rhythms, similarities and differences that meant that it just happened.' Benedict himself said that, 'when Martin walked in I just felt my game go whoop!' Gatiss was impressed with the way Freeman's dry sense of humour complemented Benedict's. 'They got on immediately . . . it just clicked.'

Even in interviews Freeman acts as the perfect deadpan foil to Benedict's exuberance. When *Den of Geek* asked if the two of them had read Conan Doyle's work before being cast in *Sherlock*, Benedict eagerly began, 'Very much I've been reading the books. It's the origination, it's the primary source. You should always go back to the books. I don't think what we're doing requires that, in particular, because it's a modern interpretation. But, you have to bring what is unique about his character to a modern context, and to do that you have to understand his original self.' Whereas Martin simply added, 'I'm a deaf mute. [Benedict] reads them out to me.'

FIRST-EPISODE FEARS

'A Study in Pink' (based on Conan Doyle's *A Study in Scarlet*) was filmed as the sixty-minute *Sherlock* pilot episode, directed by Coky Giedroyc. BBC executives liked the concept so

Instant chemistry: Benedict and Martin Freeman on set in 2013. Because every Sherlock needs his Watson (and a deerstalker).

'I came in, read with Benedict and it instantly worked
... I thought he was a fantastic actor and there
was something about our rhythms, similarities and
differences that meant that it just happened.'
— Martin Freeman

SHERLOCK

much they decided not to broadcast it – wait, this does make sense – but instead commissioned a series of three ninety-minute episodes. The story was re-filmed, this time with director Paul McGuigan at the helm (the original pilot was later released as a DVD extra).

Cast and creators had no idea what kind of reception *Sherlock* would get as they huddled round the TV at Moffat's house in Kew on 25 July 2010 to watch the first episode. The BBC had brought forward the premiere to July and all TV folk know that summer is a difficult time to nab viewers. MoffGat had even joined Twitter in an attempt to publicise the series and get viewers interested. 'It was really only one step up from individually knocking on people's doors and shouting, "Sherlock is coming!" through their letterboxes,' Mark Gatiss told Caitlin Moran in the *Times*. 'We were almost . . . desperate.' They anticipated, 'Four million viewers, tops, and a couple of nice broadsheet write-ups. That was our best-case scenario.'

As cast and crew nervously glugged their wine and waited for the show to start, they realised that something crucial was missing. Someone, in fact. Benedict had not arrived. So, as soon as the show started, they had to pause it and wait for the errant Sherlock to turn up. 'He called us – he was stuck

'It's my BAFTA and I'll frown it I want to': Sherlock and Watson get to grips with their very own bit of bronze, 2011.

Benedict enjoys cosy times with Martin Freeman and Olivia Poulet at the *Creation* premiere, September 2009.

in a traffic jam on Baker Street,' Moffat recalls, 'Sherlock Holmes, stuck on Baker Street! We couldn't work out if that was a good sign or not.' Gatiss suggests, however, that it maybe wasn't quite as poetic as all that. 'I think he might have made that up, to be honest [. . .] But it's a really good lie.' Whatever the traffic-jam truth, Benedict did eventually arrive, and the party could finally press play and watch the episode, ten minutes behind the rest of the UK. As soon as it ended, Moffat checked Twitter and realised that the internet had exploded with *Sherlock* love. #MartinFreeman, #Sherlock and, of course, #BenedictCumberbatch, were trending worldwide. Moffat realised, 'Everything had changed in 90 minutes.'

'A Study in Pink' pulled in 7.5 million viewers on 25 July – almost double MoffGat's 'best-case scenario' – with final viewing figures reaching over 9.2 million. (And that's not counting the millions of illegal downloads.) The episode was (legally) downloaded almost 1.5 million times from BBC iPlayer, becoming the third most requested programme of 2010. The Belstaff trench coat which Sherlock wears was suddenly on every fashionista's blog. It promptly sold out. Geeky weirdness and Sherlock chic was hot.

Sherlock, i.e. Benedict Cumberbatch, had arrived.

FAME GAME

Ah, fame. A vast percentage of actors spend their lives in pursuit of it, helplessly following in its wake without ever getting close enough to touch its slippery façade, while for those chosen few who do scale the walls of fame, the heavy scrutiny and loss of privacy can be a confusing, unpleasant experience. On the plus side, there's the ensuing wealth, esteem and career satisfaction – and being given heaps of free shit at Hollywood gifting suites. Still, despite those gratis Ray-Bans, Prada shoes and Ed Hardy sweatshirts, fame's undoubtedly a bit of a double-edged sword. And Benedict – definitely no twerking tween (he was in his mid-thirties by the time Sherlockian fame came a-knocking) – was well aware of the pitfalls of celebrity. Although no one could have predicted the global success of *Sherlock*, Benedict must have had some inkling that it would be life-changing, because he very nearly turned it down. He recently admitted to *Entertainment Weekly*, 'my reservation was, "Well, this is a very iconic character, there will be a lot of attention on it."' He knew the role would shake up his Cumberlife considerably. 'This was before I had had any significant success [but] I knew there would still be a lot of focus on it. And while I had done work, it wasn't stepping into the populist limelight like playing a character like Holmes. So I did have a pause for thought.'

But – thank God – the lure of working with Moffat and Gatiss proved

> 'I have become a verb, as in "I have Cumberbatched the UK audience" apparently. Who knows, by the end of the year I might become a swear word too! It's crazy and fun and very flattering.'
> – *Benedict Cumberbatch*

greater than his fears. 'I thought, "If I'm going to do this, if I'm going to step into the limelight with a large leading role of iconic status, then I might as well do it with these people." [. . .] They know what they're doing and I completely trust them. I felt like I was being asked to join the family and have some fun. There was nothing businessy about it.'

On the whole Benedict seems to be on good terms with that fickle goddess fame, managing his super-star status with just the right blend of humour and gratitude. Remember when he insisted on running up to hug Cumberbitches who'd travelled to the UK from the far corners of the Earth (well, Germany and Hong Kong) to watch him be interviewed on the *Graham Norton Show*? His generosity forced his *Star Trek Into Darkness* co-star and fellow interviewee Chris Pine to follow suit, rushing up to hug his fans (aka his 'Pine nuts'). A lovely example of Benedict's loveliness making others lovely too!

Interviewers frequently comment

Pretty fly for a genetically-engineered-superhuman guy. Benedict shows how polished he Khan look alongside *Star Trek* co-stars (from left to right): Chris Pine, Alice Eve, Zachary Quinto and Zoe Saldana.

on Benedict's politeness and the consideration he shows for everyone around him. For instance, journalist Elizabeth Day wrote in the *Guardian*, 'Benedict Cumberbatch might conceivably be the politest person I have ever met [. . .] He does seem to have a genuine, un-actorly concern for other people.' With a smile Benedict explains how he keeps it real. 'I still take public transport. I still go shopping [. . .] I don't send minions out while I sit at home at the top of a tall ivory tower with guns pointed at the street.'

So how come the B'batch hasn't started demanding peeled M&Ms and hand-juiced acai Bellinis served in the skulls of prehistoric animals wherever he goes?

Maybe it comes from having achieved fame at what (in our youth-obsessed times) is considered a mature age? He himself doesn't think so. 'Just because I'm in my thirties, it doesn't make the weirdness of no longer being private any less. I don't think it matters whether it happens when you're 25 or 55; it's just very odd. Something is suddenly taken away, and it's weird.'

Maybe it's because – unlike the perfectly symmetrical Chris Pines of this world – Benedict is still unaccustomed to being a heartthrob? He's described his look as follows: 'This face. It's kind of long. Horsey. Not as in "rah" but as in equestrian . . . It's very period, is what I'm trying to say. I'm a bit of an oddity

in a modern context. It'd be really nice to wake up looking like, I don't know, Jake Gyllenhaal and think, "Let's try this on for a day and see how it feels".' No, B'batch, *no*. Please never sacrifice your fine bone structure for Gyllencheeks. Not even for one day.

Maybe it's his intense intellect and superior acting skills that mean he knows exactly how to manipulate an audience? 'Look at you lot. You're all so vacant. Is it nice not being me? It must be so relaxing.' (OK, that was a quote from *Sherlock*, not Benedict.)

Or could it simply be that he's just a really nice guy who's happy to have achieved success at what he loves doing? This seems the most likely option. That said, there are things about fame that Benedict dislikes. As he told the *Radio Times*, he finds it frustrating when people think they know him based on, 'the trail you leave with your work [. . .] they assume things about you because of who you play and how you play them, and the other scraps floating around in the ether. People try to sew together a narrative out of scant fact.' Ah. Hmm. Luckily this book is based on very un-scant fact. Plentiful fact, in fact. (But please accept my sincere apologies if any facts turn out to be scantier than I thought them.)

Ultimately, Benedict is very *om* about his fame. 'I have been around for ten years. I don't want to complain or explain. It's a thing that will pass. It's part

5 THINGS YOU DIDN'T KNOW ABOUT SHERLOCK

(or that you did know . . . in which case you can be very Sm(a)ug!)

1. Despite the fact that Holmes is the most frequently portrayed human literary character on screen, the meeting between Holmes and Watson has never been captured on film prior to 'A Study in Pink'. (According to the *Guinness Book of World Records*, Sherlock beats the runner-up, Hamlet, by 48 portrayals. In case you were wondering, the most frequently filmed literary character – if we include *non*-humans – is Bram Stoker's blood-sucking fiend Dracula. Sherlock Holmes would almost certainly know and appreciate this factoid.)

2. In episode two, 'The Blind Banker', Benedict aced that astounding pen-toss-catch on the first take. Unfortunately there was a camera issue so it had to be re-shot. It took B'batch another three attempts to get it right. In case you're thinking that Benedict is clearly superhuman, I should point out that he *was* looking in a mirror to know when to catch the pen. (But I reckon it's still pretty impressive . . . OK, I take it all back, he's totally superhuman and could blatantly take Dracula.)

3. During filming, several Belstaff Milford wool tweed coats were used, but Mark Gatiss bought the original one used in the pilot and gave it to Benedict Cumberbatch as a gift. Aw. Fraternal love.

4. To create *Sherlock*'s lean-mean-ninja-machine look, Benedict goes on the 5:2 diet in the run up to production. During filming, his workouts include swimming and Bikram yoga, aka 'hot yoga'. He also tries to lay off smoking and drinking during the shoots (something that no doubt helps when acting out Holmes's nicotine pangs).

5. Speedy's Cafe exists! It's located on London's North Gower Street (which stands in for Baker Street in the show) and *Sherlock* fans now flock there from around the globe. Something the management cater for: fans can enjoy specially created Shersnacks, like the tasty 'Sherlock wrap'.

Speaking for the children: Benedict, Sir Ben Kingsley and friends staging *The Children's Monologues* in 2010.

of a predictable pattern.' So far there have been no discernible indications that Benedict's star is set to do anything other than rise. He's not really one to follow 'predictable patterns', is he?

ON THE BOYLE FOR CHARITY

As the star of one of the BBC's biggest successes, Benedict found the job offers – which had always been coming in at a steady pace – positively flooding his agent's office. Rather than going straight for the Hollywood movies, however, he decided to work with one of the biggest film directors of our time – but on stage.

Danny Boyle (of *Trainspotting, Slumdog Millionaire* and the London 2012 Olympic Opening Ceremony fame) first directed Benedict in 2010 at the Old Vic Theatre in London. The one-off production, *The Children's Monologues*, was performed on 14 November to tie in with World Aids Day on 1 December. It comprised a series of speeches based on the experiences of children living in abject conditions in rural South Africa. The play was dedicated to the charity Dramatic Need, which works to give children affected by trauma and hardship access to creative outlets, and raised money for the Pete Patsa Arts Centre, a South African venture where children can express themselves through crafts and drama.

Fifteen high-profile actors dedicated their time and talent to the project, including Sir Ben Kingsley, Rose Byrne, Tom Hiddleston, Romola Garai, Gemma Arterton and, of course,

Benedict. B'batch played a missionary worker trying to help a young boy who had been caught stealing. The actors and director all met for the first time on the morning of the 14th and spent eight intensive hours putting the show together.

Speaking about the project, Benedict said, 'Because they're children, they very often don't have a voice to translate or understand or communicate what they experience, so any kind of introduction to a medium where they can relate what they've experienced – I think that's great.'

A CUMBERBOYLE CREATURE

In 2011 Benedict reunited with Danny Boyle to star in one of the most popular theatrical productions of the century – *Frankenstein*. This adaptation of Mary Shelley's famous horror story about the scientist Victor Frankenstein and his unfortunate monster (sewn together from bits of corpses – ew) premiered on the main stage of London's National Theatre on 5 February 2011. Tickets sold out in record time, with the critics practically falling over themselves to lavish praise on this 'stunning' (the *Standard*, the *Telegraph*, the *Times*) new production.

The idea of a stage version of the story first occurred to Boyle in the early 1990s, but had to be put on hold while he conquered Hollywood, won Oscars, did the laundry, achieved global fame and fortune and fed the dog. (We've all been there, right?) He had always wanted to focus on the personal and social aspects of the tale, rather than the traditional 'horror' aspect popular with B-movie makers and Halloween costumers everywhere; you know, that inexplicably green-faced monster (corpses aren't green, surely?) with bolts sticking through his head, swaying from side to side, arms outstretched for ease of killing. You've probably seen him on *Scooby-Doo*.

Boyle told the *Metro*, 'Movies have done so much to distort the story. We wanted to give the creature his voice back.' For Boyle and scriptwriter Nick Dear, the 'monster' wasn't a monster, but a 'creature'. They wanted to return to Shelley's original text, which shows a more nuanced version of good versus evil, where the creature does evil because he is mistreated, rather than because he's born 'bad'. In fact, in many ways it's the scientist, Victor, who's the real baddy, the true monster of the piece. Reflecting on the life and times of Victor Frankenstein, Benedict said, 'You had this massive burst of the Industrial Revolution, which was really about electricity and the magic of light and life that gave.' On the topic of the scientist's personal reasons for creating the creature, B'batch says, 'Victor is also motivated by the death of his mother, who died caring for his cousin; he's also got a very complex relationship with

his fiancée Elizabeth, so for him there's a massive motivation to conquer death in this world of darkness [. . .] He sees himself as a hero but, by the end, it's become a suicidal pact.'

The production featured two interesting directorial decisions. The first was to film the play and broadcast it, live, to cinema audiences both nationally and internationally, enabling a whole new audience to access the play (and lending comfort to the many Cumberbitches who failed to get their hands on theatre tickets). In this way millions of people were able to see the show, making it a global phenomenon. The second decision was to have the two lead actors, Benedict and Jonny Lee Miller, alternating the roles of

Benedict appearing as the pustulant Creature (left) and then troubled Creator (right) – with Jonny Lee Miller donning the pus – in The National Theatre adaptation of Mary Shelley's *Frankenstein*, February 2011.

Victor and the Creature throughout the run of the play; one night the creator, next night the creation. Not only was this a significant challenge for Benedict and Lee Miller, but it also encouraged audiences to see the play twice to get the benefit of each actor's unique take on each of the main parts. Boyle told the *Metro*, 'The way the creature starts copying his creator is one of the key narrative drives [. . .] He is born good and learns evil. They are distorting mirrors of each other, photocopies.' Benedict told *Intelligent Life* that he found the idea of alternating roles very

> ## 'I hate this distinction of me being some fucking academic who has just managed to escape the allure of some postgraduate course.'
>
> *— Benedict Cumberbatch*

appealing. 'Danny mentioned it as a possibility in our first meeting. I said I would only be interested if that was going to happen. I think it makes such perfect symmetry to the piece, and it balances out the workload [. . .] It just keeps everything fresh; it keeps people on their toes.' He also explained what a hardcore physical experience the play was, and how it repeatedly resulted in a variety of Cumberscratches. 'We've had all sorts of injuries, back problems and neck problems. It's a hard show to do, but it's also been wonderful. Thank God I like Jonny Lee Miller.' (His 'liking' for Jonny is a sentiment he's had to reaffirm repeatedly for *Elementary* reasons to be discussed shortly . . .)

Once again tarred with the 'posh brush', Benedict was quick to dismiss any ideas about the differences between his and Lee Miller's acting processes. 'I hate this distinction of me being some fucking academic who has just managed to escape the allure of some postgraduate course, and Miller as this mad fucking wild child with dyed hair from *Trainspotting*.' Well that fucking well fucking told them, didn't it? Cooling it on the f-bombs, B'batch conceded, 'We have different working methods, but ever so slightly – we block on the same lines. We've got the same sense of humour and think much the same about what's good and bad.'

Benedict's longing for a batch of mini Cumberbabies appears to have influenced his interpretation of the *Frankenstein* tale. 'What really goes wrong in this experiment,' mused Benedict, 'is that Victor doesn't care for what he's created [. . .] I suppose you could say it's ultimately a novel about bad parenting.' Move over *What to Expect When You're Expecting*, Mary Shelley's in town . . .

ELEMENTARY, MY DEAR JONNY
While this does involve a slight fast-forward, I feel now's a good time to address the other trench-coated, scarf-wearing, slightly autistic elephant in the room: namely Jonny Lee Miller's Sherlock Holmes. Having worked with Benedict in 2011, the following year Lee Miller took on the role of the most famous detective of all time. On TV. In a modern-day adaptation. Awkward much?

Initially sources reported that Benedict was far from happy about this development, saying that Jonny had done it for the 'paycheque' after

do with the quality of the script and the challenges of this exceptional role.'

However, at the Cheltenham Literary Festival, Benedict did admit that he thought it was a calculated move on the part of the producers to cast the other Frankenstein as another Sherlock. 'Was I cynical about them going to him and asking [given that we had worked together on *Frankenstein*]? Yeah, but I've yet to go and talk to them about where their original thoughts came from to cast him, but I know for a fact that they kept on going back to him so he must have knocked it out of the park in the auditions.'

Lee Miller himself was understandably doubtful about taking on a role so obviously comparable to Benedict's; and he also worried what his other good friend, Jude Law (Rob Downey, Jr's Watson), would make of it. Benedict told Cheltenham Literary Festival (NB, this isn't the clearest of Sherlock-style monologues. Less brilliant, more, erm, garbled), 'So [Jonny] felt really nervous; he wasn't sure about it, and he asked if I was alright with it, and I said "Of course I am, of course I am," and so the thing that always gets quoted now – because people want to sell the programme off two friends who *are* friends, having a fight that they're not having because they're friends – is that: what I've said, which I haven't said, which is that I didn't want him to do it. And it's not true, I didn't. Even what I've just said

Sometimes two Sherlocks *do* make a right (but a bald Sherlock? What the Holmes?). Benedict and Jonny Lee Miller in 2011.

he'd begged him not to. However, he later told the *Hollywood Reporter* that he'd been misquoted. 'I never said that Johnny took the job for the paycheque, nor did I ask him not to do it. What I said is I would have preferred not to be in the situation where we will again be compared because we are friends. I know for a fact his motivations were to

SHERLOCK ON SHERLOCKS

Which Sherlock would Sherlock watch if Sherlock could watch Sherlock?

BC on Basil Rathbone – 'It wouldn't have appealed to me as much to play an original Holmes, because I feel that it has been done in so many ways superlatively well by Rathbone in black-and-white and by Brett in colour.'

BC on Jeremy Brett – 'I saw [the Granada series *The Adventures of Sherlock Holmes*] when I was growing up. Jeremy Brett was wonderful. He was someone who I very much remember watching play Holmes.' Benedict told the Cheltenham Literature Festival, 'Even when I was younger I was still struck by [Brett's] extraordinary hawk-like, magisterial, cold disconnect […] And this incredible physique, as well – that wonderful beak of a nose, the swept back hair, the lips and those slightly mad eyes, which, sadly, became a lot madder.'

BC on Robert Downey, Jr – 'I was quite frightened. I was, genuinely. I thought, "If I watch this, and I'm completely blown away …" but then, again, it belongs to its period, it's a different time in their relationship. They're older. […] It was great. It's a good film. But it wasn't particularly to do with what I have in mind as the original Holmes and Watson.'

BC on Jonny Lee Miller – '[He is] phenomenal; he's completely different [from my Sherlock]; he's far more contained. He's stunning to watch as well – he's just a beautiful specimen, Jonny – and he really knows what he's doing, he's completely got under his skin and it's another *Sherlock* for the 21st century.'

can now be taken out of context and used against me . . .'

Just to clarify (no quoting out of context here), Benedict and Jonny are still friends; they don't hate each other; they don't mind that they're both playing the same character (again); they're fed up of people thinking they're struggling with some irreconcilable differences (again). Basically, it's all good. This

town is big enough for the both of them. And anyway, their Sherlocks live in different towns. Different continents, in fact. (Incidentally, no word on Martin Freeman's feelings about Lucy Liu playing Watson. I'm guessing there's less risk of people confusing the two of them.)

BREAKING UP IS HARD TO DO . . .

March 2011 brought a shocking announcement: after almost twelve years together, Benedict and Olivia were ready to call time on their romance. As the news broke post-season one of *Sherlock* (in which, incidentally, Olivia plays the role of Amanda in episode two, 'The Blind Banker'), speculation was rife that it was the pressures of Benedict's newfound fame that had led to the spilt – a claim which B'batch has since vehemently refuted. In an interview with *ELLE* magazine, he opened up, saying, 'It happened very gradually, very mutually. We're still very good friends. There was no acrimony. I love her, adore her – always will.' *See?* Benedict and Olivia's romance had run its course well before *Sherlock.* Because *Sherlock* is only ever a force for good. (The TV series, that is. The man himself is more of a grey area. Which is why we love him.) Press him for further Benlivia-split details at your peril. When the *Radio Times* did some

Benedict and Olivia in happier times, namely the 2009 *London Evening Standard* Theatre Awards.

probing, B'batch fired back with: 'As much as people have conjectured, "Oh, it's typical, it's the first love being done over," well no, of course it's fucking not . . . But you know, everyone gets hold of scant facts, and because they're obsessed with me, they weave a narrative.'

And don't be expecting any Benedirt from Olivia either. 'We are absolutely grand and adore each other,' she told the *Standard.* 'Of course I am pleased for him. He has gone absolutely stratospheric and he deserves every bit of it because he's so talented and he's worked fucking hard. I couldn't think of a person who deserves it more. I always knew he was going to be huge because he was always brilliant and had that drive.'

Elementary, my dear Olivia. And, with so much Cumberlove between these two, who's to say that the Benlivia split wasn't simply a case of two university sweethearts growing up and drifting apart? As Benedict himself muses in the *Guardian,* 'When I was last single I wasn't the same person. I was desperately backwards in coming forwards. But now I quite enjoy it. Naturally, I miss the proximity of a partnership with someone I know and love . . . but being single's fun.'

MY LITTLE (WAR) PONY

It's a fairly common joke among out-of-work thespians to claim you're 'resting' whilst waiting for Steven Spielberg's call, but for newly-single

Benedict, this scenario actually came true. He'd been planning to take a break from acting. 'It sounds like a cliché, saying "I'll do that unless Spielberg calls". [But] I had literally said that about taking a break and a week later, I had to eat my words. Nobody will believe me, but there we are.'

Having been blown away by season one of *Sherlock*, Spielberg was understandably keen to work with Benedict. In an interview with *Empire*, he gushed that Benedict was the best Sherlock Holmes he'd ever seen. (Rob Downey, Jr was unavailable for comment.) Without further ado, he set about contacting B'batch's agent. Benedict naturally accepted the offer of an audience with the original Mr Blockbuster, but on the appointed date he kept the biggest bigwig in Hollywood waiting while he struggled to find a parking place for his motorbike. Benedict told the *Belfast Telegraph*, 'I went in there going, "Gosh, the first time I am meeting Spielberg and I'm apologising for being late!"" But, as fans longing for the next season know, Mr Sherlock Holmes is worth the wait. Benedict says, 'When I explained myself to him, he was fine with it. He was lovely, just lovely.' On the strength of that one – delayed – audition, Benedict

> **'I was just very bad at horse riding. It wasn't something that really took to me.'**
>
> *– Benedict Cumberbatch*

landed the role of Major Jamie Stewart in World War One epic, *War Horse*.

In this equine family film, Benedict, along with the other soldiers, wears one of those khaki army sort-of-hat, sort-of-cap things, with a peak that almost covers his eyes – all of which would make him nearly indistinguishable from co-star Tom Hiddleston if it wasn't for the fact that B'batch also sports a sandy-coloured triangular Cumbertache. While not the cutest of furry friends (it's a bit too reminiscent of Paul Marshall's rapist moustache in *Atonement*. Shudder), it certainly makes him easy to spot.

Based on the children's book by Michael Morpurgo (which has also been turned into a very successful stage play featuring big horse puppets), *War Horse* tells the story of Joey, a thoroughbred stallion, chronicling his life before and during the Great War. There has been much speculation as to whether Benedict and his co-actors Jeremy Irvine and Tom Hiddleston actually rode the horses in the film or whether they relied upon stunt doubles. For his part, Benedict doesn't want anyone thinking he left the donkeywork to someone else. To his

Sporting the definitive 'I'm-not-Tom-Hiddleston' moustache in 2011's *War Horse*.

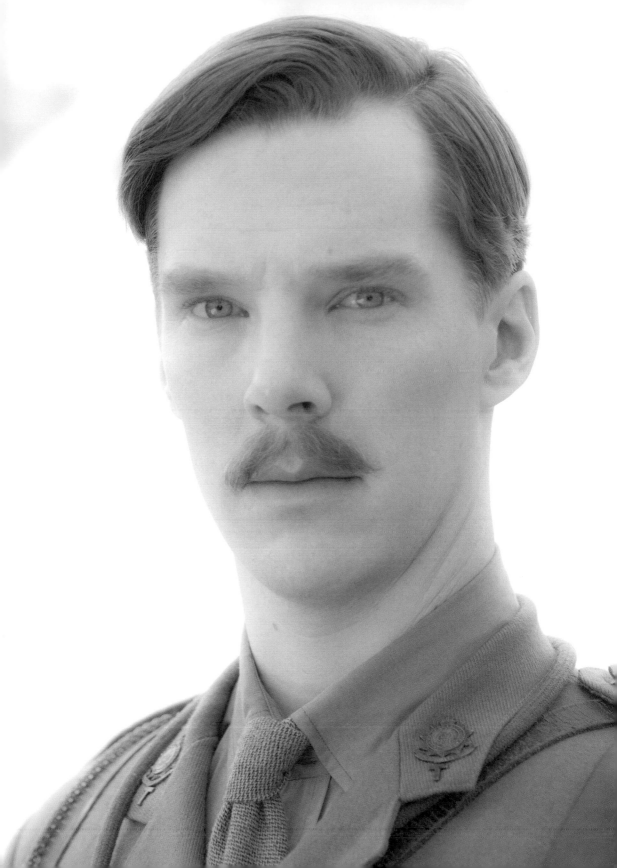

chagrin: 'People think we had our faces superimposed onto our body doubles, which is rather irritating.' While Irvine apparently excelled on horseback, Benedict – who had ridden briefly as a twelve-year-old – found it something of a struggle. The actors were given lessons to teach them how to ride one-handed while holding weapons. Nevertheless, Benedict found that, 'I was just very bad at horse riding. It wasn't something that really took to me.' Part of the problem was that, being the kind and sensitive person we stalk and love, he couldn't help but fret about the horse's feelings. Pouring out his Cumberheart, Benedict remembered how, 'I got to the stage where I thought the horse probably wanted to do something else, and I couldn't get past my awkwardness about that.' Batches of awww. Ultimately, however, Benedict now feels that the equestrian experience was less night*mare* and more *horse*play: 'A new form of relationship comes with the respect gained by getting over that. You have to be respectful of the personality of the beasts.'

COLD WAR, HOT CASH

Back when he was a well-respected-but-fairly-unknown actor, i.e. BS (Before *Sherlock*), Benedict was in talks to appear in the first ever cinema adaptation of John le Carré's famous novel, *Tinker Tailor Soldier Spy*. Then fame hit. As he puts it, '*Tinker Tailor* was a creative

> ## 'I've always wanted to play a spy, because it is the ultimate acting exercise. You are never what you seem.'
>
> *– Benedict Cumberbatch*

offer before it was a financial one [. . .] because they wanted famous people in all the roles and *Sherlock* hadn't come out. Once that was out, it suddenly became a commercial offer as well.'

However, Benedict's initial meeting with Swedish director Tomas Alfredson (who received international recognition in 2008 with vampire-flick, *Let the Right One In* – one of Benedict's favourite films) was a bit of a disaster. This time it wasn't a motorcycle-related problem; it was an issue with the script. Benedict had made it clear that he unfortunately wouldn't have time to read the *Tinker Tailor* script before his meeting with Alfredson because he was in previews for a play at the National Theatre. Unfortunately this message never reached Alfredson and when Benedict walked into the meeting at Working Title Films, 'the first thing that Tomas said to me was: "What did you think of the script?" I told him I hadn't read it and he just looked at me, mouth agape:

"You, you, you haven't read the script?" I felt awful. He was sat at this glass table at the top floor of these new offices, and there's this massive mural by Gilbert & George on the wall – a status bit of artwork – with its really bright colours showing the modern social malaise. It was all a little odd.' But it didn't take long for the B'batch charm to work on Alfredson and secure the part of Peter Guillam, a member of the Intelligence Service working with George Smiley (played by Gary Oldman) to uncover a mole within the Service. It was a dream role for Benedict, who told the *Daily Mail*, 'I've always wanted to play a spy, because it is the ultimate acting exercise. You are never what you seem.'

Spy hard: B'batch's double-crossing Peter Guillam turns his gaze on George Smiley (Gary Oldman) in 2011 slow-burner *Tinker Tailor Soldier Spy*.

As always, whether playing a real-life or fictional person, Benedict began by delving deep into his character's background. As he told the *Herald Scotland*, 'Before this story begins Guillam's a man who ran an operation in North Africa . . . Morocco probably . . . A port town, where he was a clerk and he had Arab agents. Being a French protectorate, he is fluent; he is Anglo-French, his father was French and worked in the Resistance and his mother, we think, worked in Bletchley Park.' None of this info is really relevant to an audience watching the

film, but Benedict likes to know where his characters have been, what they ate for breakfast, what underpants they wear – all the crucial stuff.

The film is definitely an actor's film – it doesn't rely on special effects or cheap thrills, this is a slow-burner of a movie with everything relying on the performances – and consequently it attracted some actor's actors. In fact, B'batch was so impressed with the calibre of his co-stars that he told a journalist, 'I'm framing my call-sheet from yesterday because it was Colin Firth, Kathy Burke, Stephen Graham, Gary Oldman, John Hurt – even John le Carré made a brief appearance. He was on this call-sheet, and I got him to

'Hey, isn't that my moustache from *War Horse?*' A clean-shaven Benedict attends the premiere of *Tinker Tailor* at Venice Film Festival 2011 – alongside a moustachioed Gary Oldman and an amused Colin Firth.

sign mine. It really was an extraordinary day at work.' Maybe, like Benedict, *all* the great actors long to play spies?

PARADE'S END

In 2012 the *Telegraph* reported that Benedict had 'fallen in love with an overweight civil servant called Christopher'. But this wasn't a Cumber-coming-out story (sorry, lads). The Christopher in question is Christopher Tietjens, the protagonist of Ford Madox Ford's tetralogy of World War One novels, *Parade's End*. Benedict was chosen to play him in Tom Stoppard's five-part TV adaptation and grew incredibly fond of the emotionally repressed anti-hero, saying 'I am enamoured of his principles, his virtue and the goodness he stands for. [. . .] I love him. I really do think that Christopher Tietjens is the character I'm most fond of ever having played.' (Whoa there, Benedict, not sure you want to invoke the jealousy of Sherlock – that could get messy.)

Christopher is caught in a love triangle with his beautiful but vindictive wife Sylvia (Rebecca Hall – who Benedict had previously worked with on *Starter for 10*) and the young, adoring suffragette Valentine (Australian actress Adelaide Clemens). In order to pull off Christopher's puffy physical appearance, Benedict underwent some serious padding to un-lean his body and also had plastic cushioning inserted into his cheeks to make them appear less hollow. He says he used London Mayor Boris Johnson 'as a visual reference' but that the production team thankfully halted him before Christopher lost all visual appeal, 'I wanted to go further with it . . . but I think they were slightly nervous about any kind of attractiveness being

'But are my cheeks big enough?' Benedict puffs up for *Parade's End*, with onscreen wife Rebecca Hall, 2012.

completely lost.' Ugh. The reduction in cheekbone boniness was bad enough; had there been *further* transformative padding, it's likely the production would have been hit by some full-on Cumberbitchin' riots.

Indeed, at this point, Benedict's behaviour resembles that of a man possessed. Even when he was sleeping, he couldn't seem to get Christopher

to you, and it looked like the image had vanished into you.' Eerie stuff, indeed – and it gets eerier. 'The next day I was [filming] a dream sequence where I'm turning in slow motion to (Tietjens' lover) Valentine. She's having this dream that turns to a nightmare. I turn to her, this explosion goes off and I'm flung back with smoke and fire, with half my face missing, spooled out on the barbed

'I really do think that Christopher Tietjens is the character I'm most fond of ever having played.'

– Benedict Cumberbatch

Tietjens out of his Cumberbrain. In a hotel where he was staying for the duration of the shoot, it seems he was visited by a ghostly spectre from the horrific battlefields of World War One. In conversation with the *Huffington Post*, he recounted all the spooky details of his very own curious incident in the night-time. 'I was asleep and my then-girlfriend woke up,' remembers Cumberbatch (and yes, Benedict did just use the 'G' word – more on this startling new development later). 'I woke up to her saying, "Are you all right?" She told me, "You were sitting on the end of the bed, and then I turned to where your voice was and you were lying down. You turned round where you were sitting and half your face was missing, you seemed to be in some sort of uniform, and just sort of vanished . . . and I looked back

wire.' Woah, talk about art imitating life. Or maybe B'batch's new ladylove had been flicking through the *Parade's End* script before bed?

Tellingly writer Tom Stoppard had been convinced for years that Benedict was his perfect Christopher and began championing him for the part even pre-*Sherlock*. However, at that stage the American backers (*Parade's End* is a co-production between BBC and HBO) had exclaimed 'Benedict, *who*?' Post-*Sherlock*, with Mr Spielberg proudly declaring himself a Cumberfan, it was considerably easier to convince everyone that Benedict was ideal casting material. In fact, HBO insisted that he play the role! 'It was a mark of

'And the award for Best Stubble goes to . . .' B'batch at the *London Evening Standard* Theatre Awards, 2009.

BENEDICT

how crazy and different things have got,' said Benedict. Um, more like 'sane and different'.

The first episode of *Parade's End* attracted 3.5 million viewers when it aired in the UK – the highest figure achieved by BBC2 since *Rome* in 2005. Critics were impressed with the series, with the *Independent*'s Grace Dent going so far as to call it 'one of the finest things the BBC has ever made'. Benedict's performance was hailed as brilliant, with Gerard Gilbert, also writing for the *Independent*, saying, 'Perhaps no other actor of his generation is quite so capable of suggesting the tumult beneath a crusty, seemingly inert surface.' Hmm, *pretty* sure that's a compliment . . .

At the Broadcasting Press Guild Benedict won the award for Best Actor, with Hall winning Best Actress and Stoppard pocketing the Writer's Award. The show was also nominated for several BAFTAs, but surprisingly Benedict wasn't on the list of nominees for Best Actor – something that many critics considered a snub. Oh well, BAFTA *F4FT4*, Benedict had the last laugh – he was off to Hollywood . . . with a beautiful new lady on his arm.

On 12 September – little more than a month after *Parade's End* aired on BBC2 – the hot new couple were ready

You shall go to the Grey Goose Winter Ball! Benedict plus platinum quiff plus Anna Jones show their support for the Elton John AIDS Foundation, London, October 2011.

to make their first public appearance: at a glitzy party hosted by *Vanity Fair* in honour of the 68th Venice Film Festival. Papped on the red carpet – looking devastatingly dapper in a black satin suit-and-tie combo – Benedict could hardly keep the smile off of his Cumberface. As for the brunette beauty by his side, Cumberbitches of the world were excited (well, sort of) to learn that, far from some pampered Hollywood starlet, B'batch had fallen for a regular girl with a real job (well, sort of – I mean, it's not like she works in Burger King). Benedict's date that evening – and the woman whom he chose to whisk away to Italy's most romantic city – was revealed to be designer Anna Jones.

As always, the *Daily Mail* claimed to have the inside story on the couple's blossoming romance: 'It's a very new relationship but it seems to be serious,' a mystery source is supposed to have commented. 'Anna really enjoys Benedict's company and they had a lovely time in Venice. Benedict has invited her to the London premiere of his new film. While he's quite private about his relationships, he is very happy with Anna. They are looking forward to spending more time together.'

So Benedict was headed off to sunny Hollywood with a gorgeous new gf by his side – just like some beautiful fairytale. I mean, if the *Daily Mail* had given the relationship its blessing, what could possibly go wrong?

CUMBERBATCH

'I realised quite early on that, although I wasn't trying to make a career speciality of it, I was playing slightly asexual, sociopathic intellectuals.'

– *Benedict Cumberbatch*

CUMBERBITCHIN'

Obviously he hates injustice, poverty, war and all the usual shizzle – who doesn't? But, aside from the obvious, what really gets Benedict's goat, grinds his gears, bugs his bears and locks his Sher?

1. Type casting – Benedict doesn't want to play one role over and over. 'I realised quite early on that, although I wasn't trying to make a career speciality of it, I was playing slightly asexual, sociopathic intellectuals.' He may have made the world fall in love with those asexual, sociopathic intellectuals, but Benedict's one batch who don't want to be put in no box. 'I've tried very hard not to be typecast as the posh character in period dramas. That's the thing I've been kicking against – to try and shift class and period and perception all the time.'

2. Posh bashing – Benedict is tired of people making assumptions about him based on his schooling – something he feels happens more in Britain than in the US. 'It's all so predictable. So domestic, so dumb. It makes me think I want to go to America.' (Can you hear that noise? It's the UK sobbing at the mere thought of losing B'batch.)

'I wasn't born into land or titles, or new money, or an oil rig.' But you were born into some pretty fantastic cheekbones and for that we salute your parents – great job, Wimothy.

3. David Cameron and the Tories – Benedict has said of the Edwardian period: 'There was a social structure that had to be adhered to … Everyone was held in their place, but what was honourable about it was that there was a duty of care from the top down. […] That shouldn't be tied in with any sort of fat-faced, flatulent Cameron effort at what Toryism – horribly – is now.'

4. Cuts to arts funding – 'Without sounding too self-important and pompous, it's very important for society to be able to reflect itself through storytelling … it's why I feel very strongly about budget cuts in the arts. Communities really do need outlets for art – whether it be galleries, libraries or theatres. It's not just the icing on the cake.'

5. *Downton Abbey* – 'Downton traded a lot on the sentiment in the last series … but we won't talk about that series because it was, in my opinion, fucking atrocious.' Bad luck, Downturd Scabby.

KING OF THE CUMBERVERSE

'I haven't done period dramas back-to-back, or really anything back-to-back. You get asked to do what you're most recently famed for, so I'm careful of not repeating myself.'

– Benedict Cumberbatch

BACK TO BAKER STREET OK, I know that when I ended the last chapter I may have implied that I was going to talk about Benedict's move to the US, but I lied. Sorry. First there's the second season of *Sherlock* to contend with.

Encouraged by the immense success of 'A Study in Pink' and the rest of S01, the BBC wasted no time in commissioning further *Sherlock*; already on 10 August 2010, less than a month

Exhaustion has never been sexier. Benedict struggles to stay awake for the duration of the Toronto International Film Festival, September 2013.

after the first episode screened, it was announced that there would be an S02. (Which was just as well because thousands of Benedict's newfound Cumberfans might well have stormed broadcasting house otherwise. Rioting would have ensued. And the Ho(l)me(s) Office would have had to get involved.)

For Benedict, revisiting the role that had made him a global heartthrob wasn't all plain sailing. He told the *Telegraph*, 'When I first went back to playing the part, it felt like a pale impression.' Obviously there's always a significant amount of pressure for the sequel to achieve – or, preferably, surpass – the success of the original, and in the case of *Sherlock* the stakes were raised further by the fact that MoffGat had chosen three of the most iconic and well-known Holmes stories for season two: 'A Scandal in Bohemia' (in which Sherlock encounters feisty potential love interest Irene Adler for the first time); 'The Hound of the Baskervilles' (maybe the most famous of all the tales, this is the one with the big killer dog – or is it?) and 'The Final Problem' (which ends with Sherlock and arch-nemesis Moriarty at the Reichenbach Falls in possibly the Best Cliffhanger Ever; or rather, Best Cliffjumper Ever . . .).

Gatiss explained the choice of stories to fans at the Kapow! Comic Con in London in 2011. 'We knew after having a successful first run that the natural order would be to do three of the most famous.'

However difficult it may have been to start with, clearly Benedict *did* manage to get back inside Sherlock's strange-but-compellingly-beautiful mind, because season two proved every bit the success its creators, producers and fans had hoped. The premiere was

> 'I'm ready to say goodbye to Sherlock, but I would miss him … It's much better to leave people wanting more.'
>
> *– Benedict Cumberbatch*

initially set for late 2011 but was pushed back to the prime of all prime-time slots: BBC One, 1 January 2012. New Year's Day is the UK's national staying-in-to-nurse-a-hangover-and-watch-the-goggle-box day, so the big TV channels compete for viewers by screening the best stuff they've got. Soz, ITV, but *Harry Potter and the Half-Blood Prince* don't stand a chance when the Beeb slaps you in the face with some brand new *Sherlock*. Final viewing figures for episode one showed that over ten and a half million people sat down to watch B'batch get his Holmes on. Once on-demand and repeat viewings were added to this figure, 'A Scandal in Belgravia' (not Bohemia), as the episode was titled, became the most watched programme of 2012.

In the run-up to season two, fans became increasingly concerned that there would be no season three. After all, in Conan Doyle's original, 'The Final Problem', it doesn't end well for Holmes . . . And Benedict failed to alleviate anyone's fears when he said in interview,

Filming *Sherlock* in Central London in April 2013, as the character he must continue to play for ever and ever and ever (unless he wants to unleash global Cumberpanic, of course).

Is this a Sherlock scarf or a B'batch scarf? Art imitating life imitating art – in wool, on the London set of *Sherlock*, April 2013.

'I'm ready to say goodbye to [Sherlock], but I would miss him [. . .] It's much better to leave people wanting more.'

The world was definitely not ready for Benedict to be saying any goodbyes. And luckily it turned out that he wasn't ready either. As soon as the end credits for the final episode of season two – 'The Reichenbach Fall' – had rolled, Moffat and Gatiss took to Twitter to impart the joyous news that a third season had, in fact, been commissioned along with the second. Bits of it had already been filmed. It seemed Benedict had been pulling our legs – both Sherlock and *Sherlock* were definitely coming back! So, all those sleepless nights were for nothing. Thanks a bunch, Cumber-MoffGat.

Sadly, as Benedict's professional profile was reaching stratospheric new heights, his personal life was about to take a serious down-turn. After mere months together, Benedict and Anna were officially on the rocks. 'You'd think he'd have no problem settling down thanks to his high-flying career and dapper looks,' mused the *Daily Mail* in customarily helpful style on 15 January. 'But Benedict Cumberbatch has become single once more after splitting from his girlfriend Anna Jones.'

This time around, the author will venture no particular break-up theories . . . especially since B'batch's half-sister Tracy Peacock has already come up with one of her own. In conversation with the *Sun*, she explained that: 'you would have to be a pretty smart cookie to keep up with him. I think that is possibly why he has trouble with girlfriends. He is such a lot like Sherlock – quick thinking, but not harsh. He's incredibly well read. In comparison to some he is quite an intellectual.' According to Tracy, B'batch is simply waiting for the right woman to come along – 'someone not in the acting profession . . . someone who was happy to hold the fort while he went off and pursued his career' – before finally settling down. I'd imagine there are a few (thousand) girls who feel they could live with that.

OK – so in the aftermath of the *Sherlock* premiere and the heartbreak of his split from Anna – we can finally go to Hollywood.

SHERLOCK

ON FIRE DOWN UNDER

Except we can't, because first we have to take a Kiwi detour so that Benedict can spend eight days 'voicing and physicalising' a dragon.

Peter Jackson's *The Hobbit* franchise was filmed in New Zealand, just like Jackson's previous J. R. R. Tolkien trilogy, *The Lord of the Rings*. PeteJack himself is a card-carrying Kiwi, but that's not the only reason he chose to film in this stunning location. Fact is, NZ is one of the few places on earth that appears naturally CGI enhanced, with its crazy mountains, lush greenery, many lakes and . . . um, furry-pawed animals introduced by settlers from afar (i.e. rabbits and hobbits). With one half of SherWat (the beautiful coupling that is Sherlock and his Watson) already bound for Middle Earth – Martin Freeman plays Bilbo Baggins, the sweet but clueless hero-hobbit of the story (he's basically Tim from *The Office* but with furrier feet) – Benedict seemed the natural choice for Bilbo's strong, greedy, scaly nemesis: Smaug the Dragon. *Sherlock* fans could hardly believe their luck and neither could Benedict. Here was a challenge unlike any he'd faced in his career to date. After all, there's nothing posh or public-school boyish about a large, avaricious, wicked, angry reptile (unless it's a politician, of course).

The sentimental value of Tolkien's original novel was another considerable draw for Benedict. As he told the *LA*

> '*The Hobbit* was a huge deal for me. It made me realise . . . you can read a book and have that much going on in your head as an imaginative world of characters and places.'
>
> – *Benedict Cumberbatch*

Times, '*The Hobbit* was a huge deal for me. |It| made me realise . . . you can read a book and have that much going on in your head as an imaginative world of characters and places. So, it sparked off my love of reading as well. It's a big book in my life, in a lot of kids' lives, and when I heard it was happening I thought, "I really need to audition for this."'

Proactive as always, Benedict took the initiative. 'I approached them. I put myself on tape. I auditioned. I was asked to audition, I guess, at some point.'

Way-back-when, it was Timothy who was responsible for getting Benedict hobbited up in the first place. 'My dad read this to me when I was a kid. I must have been about six or seven [. . .] it was a bedtime treat. This [film] is for him. I owe a lot of it to him. I don't know how much of his performance I ripped off. I can remember his Sméagol, his Gollum, was brilliant.' Bet when Papabatch was acting out *The Hobbit* he never imagined his hyperactive, skinny little son would one day play the massive dragon in one of the biggest movie franchises of all time . . . Clearly parents need to select bedtime stories very carefully indeed.

For his Smaug audition, Benedict cryptically told the *Telegraph* that he 'went a little reptile on it'. Whatever that means, he impressed not only Jackson, but also Gandalf himself, Sir Ian McKellen. When told that IMK liked his audition tape, Benedict became earnestly star-struck. His initial response: 'Has . . . has he seen it?' When further told that McKellen's exact words were 'electrifying – vocally and facially' Benedict couldn't contain his joy, bursting out with, 'Wow! I'm very flattered.' And no wonder. It's not every dragon who gets praised by an Oscar-nominee-cum-wizard-cum-legend (bet those dragons from *Harry Potter* were livid).

Ever the preparer, Benedict took his reptilian role very seriously indeed. Undaunted by the creature's mythical – and technically non-existent – status, he set about seeking alternate sources of inspiration. 'I'm starting to look at animations, and Komodo dragons at London Zoo,' Benedict revealed excitedly in interview with the *Telegraph*.

'They have some amazing ones. Snakes, too. So I've been going there to see how the skeleton moves differently, what the head movements are like.'

So how do you 'physicalise' a dragon that's going to be created by an SFX crew using CGI animation? Well, you wear a tight onesie with little balls attached to it (*très* chic); you attach motion-sensor blobs to your face – and then you writhe around looking 'totally insane' (at least, that's how the *AV Club* thought B'batch looked when behind-the-scenes footage emerged).

Benedict explained in the *LA Times* that, 'you've got a load of infrared camera sensors that pick up any motion from these little reflectors on this ridiculous gray suit. You're wearing a skull cap with a little dangly thing with a camera on, so it's high tech but it's sort of low-fi. It's not like stepping onto a set, even though those can often be dead places until something's breathed into them. You can still get some inspiration from them and locations even more so. It's a weird thing. I absolutely loved it after a minute of stepping on and feeling completely like a knob. Once you get over that bit of self-consciousness,

> '**Benedict is electrifying – vocally and facially.**'
> *– Sir Ian McKellen*

Bringing Smaugy back. Benedict smoulders on the red carpet at the Los Angeles premiere of *The Hobbit: The Desolation of Smaug*, December 2013.

it's so freeing.' Having put in hours of writhing, sneering and doing-the-worm, Benedict is understandably keen to set people straight when they refer to him as merely 'voicing' Smaug. (Apparently, 'voicing' almost never involves writhing or doing-the-worm.) Motion-capture filming sounds like a strenuous process, especially for Benedict who was shooting all his scenes solo, with full focus on him at all times. Things even got a little bit *Showgirls* at one point. As B'batch recounts, 'They built a wooden platform on stilts and they had this hardboard that they'd padded with some foam and mats and stuff and on top of that they put this sheepskin. It was literally like "Baum chicka baum baum," me up on my Smaug-y platform. I was like, "This is cool. I can slink around like a porn-star dragon."' Bring on the behind-scenes footage, please, Benedict!

Benedict is keen to point out that the SFX team found his carpet-writhing and other exertions 'very useful' and that it 'fleshed out and coloured' the dragon for them (allowing them to then actually build his flesh and colour him in – on the computer. So complex. Whatever happened to puppets? Like that big dragon puppet from *The Never Ending Story*? Wasn't he available?). But, although Benedict definitely says that he can recognise himself in Smaug, he also finds that the distance between himself and the CGI reptile results in a pleasant rest from the usual agony actors feel when watching themselves on screen. 'To be sat in an audience watching yourself is always really weird. You get very self-conscious as an actor. It takes you out of any enjoyment. No suspension of disbelief – "Ah, no, wrong choice, I could have done that differently and better. Why didn't they use the other edit?" It's very weird. But with this, it's completely different. [. . .] I can sort of see bits of [me] in those close-ups when he's one on one with Bilbo and with Thorin at the end; it's vague, but I can see underneath all those scales, the eyebrow movements and the mouth and stuff. So what I'm saying is, I can say that it's good without saying that much about myself.'

The other bonus about not having your actual face appear in the film is that you can play multiple parts. Never-the-slacker, Benedict also features as the evil Necromancer in *The Hobbit* movies. Sadly for Cumberfans, though you can hear his voice, you can never see his face. Couldn't he have played an elf or something *as well*? I reckon he'd look divine in those pointy ears. Though he himself doesn't seem to agree, saying, 'I knew I wasn't really right for a hobbit and maybe an elf, or a dwarf. It was always Smaug for me, always, always.' Ah well, bring on that behind-the-scenes carpet-rolling footage please. (FACT: This is why God invented DVD extras.)

WHAT'S YOUR CUMBERNAME?

Fed up with not being as excitingly-named as B'batch? Of course you are. Fear not. Through the following (deeply scientific) process you too can discover your very own weirdly-attractive-but-undoubtedly-silly name. And as a bonus your new nameage will consist of Benedict trivia; what more could a name want? All you need is your (current) first name, the month you were born in and a Benedict-movie preference.

The first letter of my (current) name is

A – Auburnginge
B – Baftasnub
C – Chickenex
D – Donkeywork
E – Eagleeye
F – Fittybum
G – Gunslinger
H – Horseyface
I – Iceagehead
J – Julyborn
K – Kidnappé
L – Limberlegs
M – Motioncap
N – Nappychange
O – Otterface
P – Poshbashnot
Q – Quirkyface
R – Rattigan
S – Shudderpaul
T – Tache-on-lip
U – Unastubbs
V – Violin
W – Wimothy
X – Xraybrain
Y – Yogayear
Z – Zoombiking

Month you were born in:

Jan – Chelsea
Feb – Dragon
Mar – LAMDA
Apr – Harrow
May – Bombthreat
Jun – Hiddle
Jul – Drama
Aug – Horsey
Sep – Carpet
Oct – Actor
Nov – Broody
Dec – Arty

Favourite B'batch film:

The Hobbit: The Desolation of Smaug – Crab
Star Trek Into Darkness – Khan
Atonement – Creep
The Fifth Estate – Leak
War Horse – Hoof
Stuart: A Life Backwards – Beat
The Other Boleyn Girl – Cheat
12 Years a Slave – Caught
Tinker Tailor Soldier Spy – Fringe
August: Osage County – Woe

YES, YOU KHAN!

Finally Benedict landed in Hollywood to live the dream of all British actors in LA: playing the bad guy. But B'batch's shot at baddydom didn't involve playing a weedy posh-guy psycho-Brit flanked by beefcake minions; nor was he a crippled evil genius stroking a Persian cat, sipping Earl Grey and plotting to end the world – no such predictability for Benedict. He chose to launch himself in Hollywood by playing Khan Noonien Singh, a genetically modified 'superman' and the ultimate *Star Trek* bad guy.

character I'm playing, he's strong [. . .] I've changed my physique a bit, so that requires eating like a *foie gras* goose, well beyond your appetite. And, providing I don't feel too ill, I then work out two hours a day with a phenomenal trainer. It's the LA way.' Ah, eatin' the dream.

As so often for Benedict, the Trekkie audition process was . . . unconventional. This time it also involved a cultural lesson in the differences between the UK and USA film industries. Just before Christmas 2011 Benedict was told he needed to put himself on tape

> 'I've changed my physique a bit, so that requires eating like a foie gras goose – well beyond your appetite. And, providing I don't feel too ill, I then work out two hours a day with a phenomenal trainer.'
>
> – Benedict Cumberbatch

Used to UK shoots in glamorous locations like, um, Wales, all the amenities of a Hollywood movie certainly appealed to Benedict, especially as he beefed up considerably for the role. Gone was the Sherlockian 5:2 diet, now he was free to nom his way through California's finest cuisine. When reporter Kate O'Hare asked if he was enjoying the on-set catering, B'batch replied, 'Yeah, you betcha. It's great. I've gone up two suit sizes. The

Looking totally Spock-tacular as Khan in *Star Trek Into Darkness*, March 2013.

and send it over to director/producer J.J. Abrams ASAP. Not asap, but ASAP. As in, DO IT NOW NOWNOW! PREFERABLY YESTERDAY! But none of his casting director contacts were around – everyone in the UK was busy with yuletide festivities. But the pressure from Hollywood to get the tape sent over didn't stop for Christmas trees, peppermint sticks or Ol' Saint Nick – so B'batch became increasingly panicked. He finally ended up at the home of his friend, actor Adam Ackland and his wife Alice, who agreed

KHAN

to help out as best they could. Benedict explained to the *New York Times*, 'My Flip [camera] wasn't working, I couldn't get any kind of recording device. I said, "I'm going to do it on my iPhone. It's high quality, it's HD. It will be fine." And so I ended up squatting in their kitchen, at about 11 o'clock at night. I was pretty strung out, so that went into the performance.' He describes the makeshift set up, with Adam filming and Alice, 'balancing two chairs to get the right angle on me and desk lamps bouncing light off bits of paper, just trying desperately to make it look half-decent. Because it's going to go into J.J. Abrams's iPad. So we did it, and then it took a day and a half to compress it. I sent it to him, and then I got told, "J.J.'s on holiday." I was furious. And then I heard on the day after New Year's Day – [. . .] he just sent me an e-mail, going, "You want to come and play?" I said, "What does this mean? Are you in town; you want to go for a drink? I'm English. You've got to be really straight with me on this. Have I got the part?"'

He had.

NEUTRONED OUT

Once on the set of *Star Trek Into Darkness*, Benedict's earnest nature led to much amusement amongst his co-stars, especially Chris Pine and UK comedy legend Simon Pegg. The latter played a particularly elaborate prank on several cast members, including Zoe Saldana,

John Cho, Zachary Quinto and Karl Urban – none of whom fell for it harder than Benedict. As B'batch explains, the punking took place while the team were filming, 'in a really futuristic laboratory with lasers that were trying to split a target smaller than a human hair to create a continual form of energy'. Benedict was in awe of the complex equipment. 'I was like "wow, this is the real deal – what can't we touch? What's safe?"' That's when Pegg and Pine got the entire cast and crew to help them prank Cumber-Khan in such a manner that Graham Norton could only conclude, 'this does make you sound like a moron'. (B'batch took this statement in good humour, admitting, 'I should have known. They had me, they completely had me.')

The big Cumberprank involved everyone on set telling Benedict that he needed to take some fairly elaborate precautions in order to remain safe in the lab. B'batch told *The Graham Norton Show*, 'I got on set and was told I needed to wear "neutron cream" to protect me. I was gullible and did what I was told; it's America and there is a lot of health and safety.' Chris Pine elaborated, 'We told him he had to apply the cream in dots all over his face and there he was doing this really intense scene with sunscreen spots all over him.'

The *STID* cast and crew at the London premiere, May 2013. Anyone else feeling a tad uneasy that they're not appropriately dressed for travel in this spacecraft? Um, health and safety regulations?

Benedict was also told that it was important to de-neutronise regularly. 'To get the neutrons off of you, you have to jump up and down and shake.' As everyone from J.J. Abrams to the assistant director to make-up artists to sound crew was in on the joke, Benedict had no reason to suspect it was a prank; he saw the others supposedly shaking off their neutrons and didn't think anything of it. Of course, he followed suit. He says, 'My science teacher's sitting at home now saying, "See, I told you." I should have paid attention rather than farting around and acting.'

If you want to see footage of Benedict farting around and acting with neutron

'Beam me up, Benny': at the London premiere of *Star Trek Into Darkness*, B'batch is more than happy to oblige.

cream (aka sunscreen) dotted around his face, it's included in the behind-the-scenes footage on the *Star Trek Into Darkness* DVD. (Or you Khan YouTube it.)

Further on-set shenanigans have been captured on the Instagram account of London-born actress Alice Eve, whose character (the imaginatively named 'Carol' . . . That is nowhere near as good as 'Spock' or 'Khan Noonien Singh', or even 'Commander Beverly Crusher, M.D.') was written into the Trekkie-verse especially for *Into Darkness*. Those able to withstand the pangs of jealously can still log on to witness the actress's numerous selfies with Benedict. For instance, you can see his perfect, smiling Cumberface reflected in novelty pink sunshades, or peeking out totes adorbs from beneath a dragon hat at Glastonbury. Oxford-educated Alice is clearly smart enough to recognise a Cumbercatch when she sees one. 'Benedict wants to have a family and I think that's what women respond to,' she said in a promotional interview for the movie. 'The thing about him is that he'll actually be a good dad and a good husband. I think he'll be loyal and he'll be caring, and women respond to that.'

But don't get too jealous, Cumberfans: it seems unlikely that these two – who first appeared together in *Starter for 10* way back before Hollywood came a-calling – were ever anything more than friends. Depressingly, however, this may be due to a certain other lady in Benedict's life: stunning heiress, supermodel, actress and-all-round-It-girl Lydia Hearst-Shaw. Lydia's beauty and more-fascinating-than-fiction family history – back in the '70s her kidnapped mother Patty was brainwashed into robbing a bank – was clearly more than Benedict could resist. In a sultry photo-shoot for *Marie Claire UK*, the chemistry between the two positively sizzled, igniting jealous

No time for jetlag: Benedict greets an army of adoring fans at Narita Airport, Japan, in July 2013 – with a string of *Star Trek* screenings ahead of him.

No need to give Alice the Eve-il eye; she and Benedict are just good friends, attending a *Star Trek* preview at London's BFI IMAX.

Yet, little more than a month after his split from Anna, Benedict seemed characteristically reticent to either confirm or deny the rumours. His management had this to say on the subject: 'They have been friends a while now, but to say they are dating is probably too strong.' Hmm, what's weaker than 'dating'? Celebrities who've never even *met* each other have been accused of dating (remember the supposed Harry Styles/Princess Anne dating scandal? No, nor do I. I just made it up.)

Much like the whereabouts of Irene Adler, the true story of Lydia and Benedict — and why this handsome Cumbercouple never really took off — will remain a mystery. Several months on, the tabloids were abuzz with reports of the actor's new 'new love interest' — and this time around it was a romance made in Middle Earth. 'Benedict Cumberbatch and Liv Tyler spark dating rumours after cinema outing,' read the *Daily Mail*'s semi-hysterical headline on 26 September. Apparently, the camera-shy pair — dressed down in matching black jeans — 'attempted to keep their distance as they strolled out of the Arclight Cinema'. Nevertheless, it was duly noted that 'they both appeared to be in good spirits following the movie'.

Is this the expression of a man so baffled by his luck that he forgot to shave? B'batch strikes a pose with heiress Lydia Hearst-Shaw at a *Vanity Fair* party in LA, January 2012.

fires in the hearts of Cumberbitches worldwide. On 29 February, they were photographed together at the 20th Annual Elton John Aids Foundation Oscar Academy Awards viewing party (and then at several other improbably-named Hollywood bashes). Though they were the talk of the town, it's clear from the pictures that the pair only had eyes for one another (exhibit A: Benedict's Cumberarm wrapped protectively around Lydia's waist).

'I've punched well above my weight this year.

And that remains very much a secret ...'

— *Benedict Cumberbatch*

I guess they saw a comedy? Because, sadly – who doesn't adore the idea of the ethereal Arwen smauggling up to a fiery but misunderstood dragon? – Benedict's rep stated emphatically that the two 'are not dating'.

Yet, Benedict himself did nothing to silence the gossip-merchants. Towards the end of 2012, he made the coy admission that, 'I've punched well above my weight this year. And that remains very much a secret . . .' Clearly, Cumber-bachelorhood suits him well.

B'BATCH O'CLOCK

Cumberbitches have always had unlimited time for Benedict and in 2012 it turned out that the *world* was a Cumberbitch. In a public poll to pick one person out of 150 nominees to nab the final spot on the *TIME* '100 most influential people in the world' list – the other ninety-nine had already been chosen by the editors of the legendary magazine – Benedict came seventh. That in itself is pretty impressive, but even more impressive (or absurd, depending on your POV) is the list of people he beat: UK Prime Minister David Cameron, Queen Elizabeth II and President Barack Obama. (Oh, and he also beat Ryan Gosling. By a long way . . . which some might consider even more of an achievement.)

Benedict received the news of his influential status with a charming blend of wit and humility, saying, 'Apparently I beat the leader of the free world. How do you like that? It's ridiculous. I'm slightly flattered. It might be an alphabetical thing. It's crazy. It's really crazy.' He also relayed that a friend had joked, 'Are you running for President?' But then he brought some lovely B'batch earnestness to the table. 'There are lots of people I'd put ahead of myself, and that's not me being humble. Come on, you know what it's about. It's flavour-of-the-month stuff, and that scares me as much as it thrills me. I'm 35, and I've been doing this for ten years. The point is, I thought, maybe I should start to do something with this moment. It's kind of inspiring in a way, because you look at it and think, "I'm not really worthy of my entry in this." It's bizarre and humbling and silly, rather than something to frame and look at and take very seriously.' Yeah and then there's the whole you-can't-be-President-of-the-US-unless-you-were-born-there thing, which is really going to hurt Benedict's presidential campaign. But he *could* run for Prime Minister of the UK . . . (Or Governor of California now Arnie's gone back to making movies.)

The Benedict entry for the *TIME* poll opened in a rather convoluted way: 'Britons might be forgiven for thinking human cloning had already proved successful. How else to explain the ubiquity of an actor whose name is only slightly less angular than his face?'

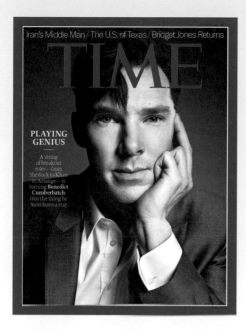

'Apparently I beat the leader of the free world. How do you like that? It's ridiculous. I'm slightly flattered. It might be an alphabetical thing. It's crazy ... really crazy.'

– *Benedict Cumberbatch*

B'batch o'clock: the legendary face graces the legendary magazine. About time, wouldn't you say?

To which Benedict's response was, 'Crikey. I think it's much less angular than my face. It's all vowels. If my face was letters, it'd be consonants, I think – apart from my nose, which is a bit blobby. It might be an O or something.' Anyone who can assign letters to match their facial features is clearly afflicted by excess energy and should be running a country. Vote Sherlock!

Which is sort of what *TIME* Magazine ended up doing in October 2013 when they put Benedict on the cover of their international edition, all to tie in with the release of Julian Assange-opic, *The Fifth Estate*. Nice attempt to try and make out it's a weighty political decision to have a Cumbercover, *TIME*

editors. But we totally know it's because you're all massive Cumberbitches.

Only the weightiest stars make it onto the front of this most iconic of mags; an actor basically has to be an icon in his or her own right to see their face splashed beneath the *TIME* logo. Former cover stars include the likes of Marilyn Monroe, Elizabeth Taylor, Tom Hanks, George Clooney, Arnold Schwarzenegger, Tom Cruise, Nicole Kidman – and now the B'batch. This ain't the place for flash-in-the-pan one-hit-wonders – once *TIME* finds time for you, you're here to stay.

BOTTLE BLOND AMBITION
The day before filming began on WikiLeaks biopic, *The Fifth Estate*, Benedict received a letter from himself.

Sort of. Well, from the person he was about to play: WikiLeaks founder Julian Assange. Holed up in the Ecuadorian Embassy in London in order to escape extradition to Sweden to stand trial for multiple rape charges, the controversial figure – responsible for releasing documents about the Iraq invasion and other sensitive issues – turned out to be a bit of a Cumberfan. Keen as always to do his research, B'batch had contacted Assange's team well in advance of filming, hoping to arrange a meeting with the blondest man in Ecuador. But he heard nothing until right before the first 'action!' was about to sound, when Assange finally wrote back. 'My assistants communicated

Pale has never been so interesting: Benedict as Julian Assange, alongside chipmunkesque Daniel Brühl in *The Fifth Estate*, 2013.

your request to me, and I have given it a lot of thought and examined your previous work, which I am fond of.' (*Such* a Cumberbitch.) He went on to acknowledge that, 'The bond that develops between an actor and a living subject is significant.' Yet he did not agree to a meeting. Instead he urged Benedict to drop out of the movie as he felt it wasn't going to be an accurate portrayal of events, but rather a damaging attack on himself.

He went on to say, 'I believe that you are a decent person, who would not naturally wish to harm good people in

'I've never been an activist, but I've always been politically aware.'

– Benedict Cumberbatch

dire situations.' Clearly keen to drum home his Benelove, he reiterated, 'I believe you are a good person, but I do not believe that this film is a good film.'

Receiving this vehement call to abandon the role he'd spent months preparing for was obviously uncomfortable for Benedict, who had been hoping for his character's blessing. He was not looking to participate in Assange assassination of any kind – there is much that he admires about the complex self-proclaimed political refugee. And B'batch didn't feel the script was biased, despite being based on two books about WikiLeaks which Assange himself considers poisonous.

With this in mind, Benedict decided to push on with the film as planned.

As it turns out, Assange probably needn't have worried because *The Fifth Estate* doesn't dwell on the rape charges against him or the Ecuadorian asylum. Instead, it focuses on Assange's relationship with friend and WikiLeaks co-worker Daniel Domscheit-Berg (author of one of the books which formed the basis for the film). As the movie progresses, their falling-out is depicted without ever really giving much insight into WikiLeaks itself. Politically

the movie is more on the fence than the offense. All in all, it was not considered a critical or a public success, though the performances – Benedict's albino-Aussie transformation in particular – were highly praised by several critics. The general consensus seems to be, however, that the script and direction could have been better, and that if you want to learn anything significant about Wiki-Leaks you'd be better off watching the documentary *We Steal Secrets,* which was released at roughly the same time. Writing for nonfics.com, Daniel Schindel summarises as follows: 'Both movies are problematic. But *We Steal Secrets* is far and away the better prospect. [. . . It] actually gives the audience a good crash course in the history of WikiLeaks and the misdeeds that it exposed.' If, however, you want to see Benedict with bleached eyebrows, *The Fifth Estate* is obviously a must. (It should be pointed out that Assange himself isn't a fan of *We Steal Secrets* either. If you want to please him you'll need to watch the WikiLeaks-funded *Mediastan,* about WikiLeakers travelling through Asia and campaigning for freedom of information.)

If you're wondering how Benedict

'I wanted to portray human characteristics about a man at the forefront of an incredible media revolution.'

– Benedict Cumberbatch

felt about dying his hair luminous – he didn't. It's a wig. He described the faux-thatch to the *Huffington Post*, 'I had a kind of skunky badger thing with the white hair [. . .] I quite enjoyed putting the wig on.' He was less of a fan of changing his eye colour, though. 'The harder thing was the contact lenses because I've never worn them before.'

When it comes to the political aspect of the movie, Benedict has some strong views about the war in Iraq. He told *TIME* Magazine, 'I've never been an activist, but I've always been politically aware. I protested against budget cuts and cuts to education. I marched against the Iraq War. All that protesting was just

swept aside to pave the way for an illegal war, and the results of that war were made very, very plain by those leaked war logs.' Consequently he has a lot of respect for Assange. As he told the *Huffington Post*, 'It was important for me to portray him as a three-dimensional human being and not get into a slagging match about whether he was good or bad. I wanted to portray human characteristics about a man at the forefront of an incredible media revolution.'

On a lighter note (*The Fifth Estate* itself really doesn't have many), Daniel Brühl, the German actor who plays Domscheit-Berg, has a Sherlockian recollection of his initial encounter with B'batch, as reported in the *Radio Times*. 'The first time I met [Benedict] in London for rehearsal, he took one look at me and told me what I had had for breakfast [. . .] And I said, "Hi, Sherlock, nice to meet you." And he said, "Sorry, sorry. I just can't let go of that part."'

BRINGING SEXYBATCH

While Cumberbitches have long been aware of the intense hotness of the Cumberface and Cumberbody, it was only in 2013 that Benedict's status as the World's Sexiest Movie Man was made official. In a poll of around 50,000 cinemagoers, conducted by top film magazine *Empire*, he nabbed the top spot,

Blue is the warmest colour: Benedict gets his pose on in Canada at the Guess Portrait Studio, Toronto International Film Festival, September 2013.

beating the likes of more conventional pin-ups Johnny Depp, Ryan Gosling, Brad Pitt, Tom Hiddleston and Henry 'Superman' Cavill.

Benedict received the news of his latest title with customary grace, saying, 'It puts a bit of a spring in your step [. . .] It's nice, you swagger a little bit, it's enjoyable [. . .] I find it hysterically funny . . . It's a giggle. I wield it with a massive smile.'

At last, B'batch was getting the recognition he so richly deserved . . . and he wanted the world to know it. In an interview at Cheltenham Literary Festival in 2013, he decided to set the record straight about his prowess as a lover. 'I always seem to be cast as slightly wan, ethereal, troubled intellectuals or physically ambivalent bad lovers. But I'm here to tell you I'm quite the opposite in real life. In fact I'm a fucking fantastic lover.'

One girl who'd surely corroborate his story is Katia Elizarova – a Russian ballerina-turned-model who has been lucky enough to be wined and dined by the Batch. The pair were first spotted together in 2012, enjoying a dinner date in Knightsbridge, London. More than a year later, she was apparently still on B'batch's mind. In July 2013, he was

> ## 'I'm here to tell you … I'm a fucking fantastic lover.'
>
> *– Benedict Cumberbatch*

set to officiate the marriage (is there *nothing* Benedict can't do?) of two of his dear friends, Seth Cummings and Rob Ridner. 'It's a very private, lovely thing to be asked to do,' Benedict told *Vulture* of his role in the upcoming ceremony. Held high in the sundrenched mountains of the island of Ibiza, Seth and Rob's special day – as captured in a selection of pictures posted online – looks nothing short of idyllic. And Katia was the lucky girl invited to share it with B'batch the Marriage Officiator.

Sick-makingly romantic pictures of the two locked in a passionate embrace in the sun are testament to just how much fun they had on the famous party island. Katia herself had this to tell the *Times*: 'He's a fantastic man. It was a wedding, you know, everyone was jolly and happy and, you know, things happen . . .' Well, not really, Katia. I've never been to a wedding officiated by Benedict Cumberbatch. But do go on. (She didn't go on.)

Just imagine it – no crusty vicar or mumbling registrar, these wedding guests had a private B'batch performance! The *Metro* reported that Benedict had promised: 'Of course I'm going to make a joke after

BENEDICT

[the ceremony] if it goes well . . . "I do weddings. Next will be children's parties and bat mitzvahs.'" In common with his onscreen alter-ego (remember Sherlock's epically awkward speech at Watson's wedding?) Benedict was apparently suffering from a slight case of pre-ceremony nerves. 'It's a mainly Jewish and gay audience so hopefully they will be lenient towards me,' he told the *Daily Mail*.

It seems as though he needn't have worried, however. At least one guest at the exclusive Hacienda Hotel ceremony, writer Julie Burchill, was absolutely charmed. 'The hotel was lush,' she raved. 'The bridegrooms were beautiful and the man who married them to each other was Benedict Cumberbatch – so yes, it was quite a blast.'

After the wedding ended, Benedict stayed on for further fun in the sun with Katia. Eschewing the 2013 San Diego Comic Con (so as not to disappoint his Cumberpublic, he filmed a heartfelt video message – cheekily teasing fans with the promise of 'Empty Hearse' spoilers), the pair were papped smooching on a poolside sun lounger. Though Benedict himself had yet to confirm the romance publicly, it was surely just a matter of time . . . wasn't it?

For the above-mentioned Katia-esque reasons, Benedict's birthday antics in London – a matter of days after he parted company with his Ibiza squeeze – caused quite the stir back in

Benedict and companion hot-foot it out of London's infamous Cirque du Soleil on 27 July 2013. The au-burning question was: who could she be?

Blighty. Just over a week after he turned 37 (on 19 July, aka National B'batch Day), Benedict was spotted out on the town with an eclectic posse of celebrity pals, including *Sherlock*-obsessed Stephen Fry, kooky designer Matthew Williamson (who painted half his face with skeletal make-up specially for the occasion) . . . and one mystery woman in black. Keeping her face hidden behind her long auburn locks, she never let go of Benedict's Cumberhand. By all accounts, B'batch and his pals had

CUMBERBATCH

spent the evening partying hard at London's exotic, opulent Cirque du Soleil. According to the *Mirror*, the rabble-rousing group 'downed vodka and Cristal and Dom Pérignon (with obligatory birthday sparklers), as they played beer pong and enjoyed a burlesque show featuring topless girls, dwarves, fortune tellers, dancing dogs and fire eaters.' Oh, Benedict . . . don't you remember what happened when Sherlock met those knife-throwers? Beware of circuses.

Days later, however, it emerged that B'batch's redheaded companion was none other than *Dracula* actress Charlotte Asprey – one of Benedict's oldest and dearest friends from LAMDA. Who is not dating Benedict, but actually living happily with her businessman boyfriend. So, tabloid journalists everywhere, in the words of Sherlock Holmes, 'Do your research!'

OKLAHOMABATCH

It was on the set of *August: Osage County* that Benedict got to work with one of his biggest fans. Her name is Meryl Streep. Yep: her of the eighteen academy award nominations. In a video on the *Independent* website, Streep says, 'I hadn't ever met [Benedict] before and he was such a gift to the film [. . .] he plays someone completely different from all the other performances we've seen and he's very tender and wounded and bruised and tentative.' (Hmm, sounds like a cuddly toy trapped in a dishwasher. #BenedictCareBearBatch, anyone?)

August: Osage County is the screen adaptation of Tracy Letts's Pulitzer Prize-winning play of the same name. This darkly-comedic family drama centres round the terminally ill – and terminally mean – matriarch Violet Weston (played by M-Streep). Fleshing out the ridiculously starry supporting cast of daughters, husbands and cousins were: Julia Roberts, Juliette Lewis, Abigail Breslin, Ewan McGregor and, of course, B'batch himself. Benedict plays against type as the mild-mannered, woefully down-trodden Little Charles, showing that he can do sweetly-shy and awkward every bit as well as Sherlock-savvy and capable. Furthermore . . . he gets to sing! You can hear B'batch exercising his pipes on an adorable ballad called 'Can't Keep It Inside'. (Included on the soundtrack, this song is 100 percent downloadable as an MP3.)

As per usual, Benedict's path to *Osage* – and the part of Little Charles – was anything but . . . um, usual. Director John Wells was quoted in the *Metro*, explaining how B'batch won the role. 'I have to confess I didn't know Benedict's work at all. He sent in a video – recorded on an iPhone – and he must have filmed it himself because you could see that it was being held at arm's length, like a selfie.' Of course he did. 'I was really taken with his talent. It was a beautiful audition.' Of course it was. Though he'd been considering several other actors for the role, Wells told the *Sun* that 'none of them had the warmth and humanity of Benedict in the part.' Of course they didn't!

B'batch masters the US accent brilliantly; don't take my word for it, here's what Meryl Streep has to say on the matter. 'He fit into this Oklahoma family effortlessly – I was surprised to learn he was British!' To obtain the Streep's seal of approval, you'd have to be pretty much perfect. (A mistress of diction who managed to portray British PM Margaret Thatcher, she definitely knows her tom-ah-toes from her to-may-toes.) Though it could, of course, be down to the fact that she didn't actually hear Benedict speak. Apparently he was too in awe of her to sustain a conversation. Yup, apparently the set of *Osage* was one big mutual adoration society. Benedict was quoted in the

Overload of aww: B'batch and Julianne Nicholson being cute in *August: Osage County*, 2013. (Not pictured: Meryl Streep writhing around on floor.)

'I know I've ruined your life, but here – take this violin!' Benedict and Chiwetel Ejiofor in 2014's harrowing epic, *12 Years a Slave*.

Argus, explaining how he got Meryl-ly tongue-tied in the presence of his idol. 'We had one scene around the table with Meryl and I just couldn't act. I was in awe of her. She is spellbinding to watch. She really is extraordinary. If you ever have the luck to watch her, she is fantastic.'

SLAVING AWAY

Not content with being in just one of the big award-magnet movies of 2013-'14 (*August: Osage County* was nominated for Oscars, Golden Globes, SAG Awards, BAFTAS – all the major hunks of metal), Benedict also crops up in Steve McQueen's slave-trade biopic, *12 Years a Slave*. (NB this particular Ste-McQ is not to be confused with the actor from *The Great Escape*; he's the British director who made Michael Fassbender get very, *very* naked in *Shame*.)

The movie tells the true story of Solomon Northup (played by Brit actor Chiwetel Ejiofor), a musician and free black man from Saratoga Springs, New York, who was abducted and sold into slavery in the 1840s. What follows is a devastating tale of cruelty and abuse, based on Northup's autobiography.

Benedict plays William Ford, the 'nice' slave owner (well, 'nice' in comparison with the sadistic whip-wielding monster, Edwin Epps, played by Fassbender – who manages to be even creepier than Paul shudder-shudder Marshall). Ford grows to like Northup, treats him with kindness and gives him a violin to play. Ultimately, however, he's too weak-willed to stand up for the rights of his slaves and sells Northup on to the abominable Epps.

The film has been lauded by critics and cinemagoers alike and is currently vacuuming up awards, with more metal gongs to come. While Benedict's performance in *12 Years* has been favourably reviewed, most of the Benepress surrounding the film has focused on the questionable heritage of his Caribbean forebears, with media outlets such as *DNA India* reporting that 'A NYC cop [. . .] recently revealed that Cumberbatch's fifth great-grandfather owned her ancestors on an eighteenth-century sugar plantation on Barbados.' The *Daily Mail* published a detailed article about the Cumberbatch slaves, mentioning that, 'New York's newly-appointed transport commissioner, an African-American lawyer named Wanda Cumberbatch, was asked at a press conference about her distinctive surname. She said that she and Benedict were "related, but not by blood," since her ancestors had taken the name of their former masters after being freed.' The article includes pictures of the Cleland Plantation which, in the seventeenth and eighteenth centuries, was owned by the Cumberbatch family and, 'was home to 250 slaves, who lived and died in conditions of unimaginable brutality'. After the abolition of slavery, 'Benedict's line of the family [. . .] dispose[d] of their Barbados land holdings [. . .] after receiving more

than £6,000 – a relative fortune – in government compensation for the loss of their human "property". By the time of a 1913 census of the island, not a single plantation was owned by a Cumberbatch.'

The present-day owner of Cleland, Stephen Tempro, had this to say on the topic of B'batch and his forebears: 'It's fascinating to think that a movie star, in a film about slavery, descends from ancestors of this particular plot.'

Moving away from murky ancestral Cumber-history to the present day, one thing B'batch definitely enjoyed about filming *12 Years* was being allowed to keep his natural hair colour, giving his scalp a rest from wigs, dyes and chemical treatments. Thankfully the makeup crew didn't model his looks too closely on the real William Ford, as that would have involved a long raggedy white beard, a fat suit – and baldness. (*12 Years a Shaven Head*, anyone? It's truly not the most desirable of Bene-looks.)

CARTOONS AND MUPPETS

Now for something much more sunny. Well, yellow anyway. In 2013 Benedict got to tick off another item on the Things-You-Get-To-Do-When-You're-Really-Kinda-Famous list when he made like Dustin Hoffman, Sting, Anne Hathaway, Meryl Streep, Winona Ryder, Ricky Gervais plus countless other celebs before him, and appeared in an episode of *The Simpsons*.

For all those wondering how Benedict came to land a cameo in the iconic animated series, *InStyle* magazine provided the inside story. (SPOILER: it's not conventional casting. In case you were worried there'd be a break with Cumbertradition.) Benedict happened to be in a meeting at the same studios where *The Simpsons* voiceovers are recorded. When he heard there was a part up for grabs, he wasted no time in throwing his hat into the ring. 'I said, "I hate to muscle in here, guys, but could I record it?" Next thing, I'm standing in a room with all those famous voices: Bart, Marge, Homer, Lisa.' The episode in question was a Valentine's Day special entitled, 'Love is a Many-Splintered Thing'. Benedict plays two parts – the British Prime Minister and Severus Snape – in a send up of the movie *Love Actually*. The episode is not considered to be one of *The Simpsons'* finest – with Rob H. Dawson of *TV Equals* dubbing it, 'completely boring and unsatisfying' – but it's definitely worth a watch, if only for Benedict's inspired impersonations (a Cumberfan's dream, you'll hear him get both his Hugh Grant and his Alan Rickman on).

February 2014 marked the ticking of yet another box on the Bene-bucket list of awesomeness, with Cumberbatch finding out first-hand how to get to Sesame Street. Yes, a short video – posted on YouTube by PBS – sees Benedict accosted by the fluffiest of arch-nemeses, Murray-arty, who sets him a dastardly difficult fruit challenge. Luckily B'batch receives first-rate assistance from the street's resident numbers guy, Count von Count.

The best thing to come out of this encounter is surely an adorable photo of B'batch – grinning from ear-to-ear like an excitable schoolboy – with Murray and the Count. Marty Freeman, beware – you could well be facing *Sherlock*-sidekick competition from these two fluffy pretenders . . .

SHERLOCKED AGAIN (AGAIN)

On 1 January 2014, Benedict – once again slimmed-down and long-of-coat – Sherlocked his way back onto UK TV screens in the first episode of season three, 'The Empty Hearse'. For a legion of Bene-starved Cumberbitches, his return to Baker Street came not a moment too soon. By this time, they'd been waiting a whole two years to find out how on earth Sherlock survived jumping from a very tall building, crashing to the very hard ground and being pronounced very, very dead in front of the very teary eyes of Watson. Their appetite had been whetted a few weeks previously by a so-called 'mini-episode' of *Sherlock* released online by the BBC on 24 December 2013. (Given that it's all of seven minutes and twelve

Just like tomorrow, Sherlock never dies. Here he is, back from the grave and filming series three, dandily deerstalkered in London, 2013.

seconds long, I'm thinking 'mini' is a tad on the baggy side; 'tiddly' might be more accurate.) Entitled 'Many Happy Returns', it features a grief-stricken Dr Watson struggling to come to terms with the death of Sherlock. The super-sleuth, meanwhile, is very much not-dead . . . and kicking – in a variety of exotic locations.

For fans looking forward to finally discovering the secret of Sherlock's faux-death, the mini episode gave precious little away. Hence, expectations for 'The Empty Hearse' were running high. Polarising Sherfans everywhere, the episode ultimately proved either an unexpected trove of treasures, or an immensely disappointing cop-out, depending on exactly who you chose to ask. Once again occupying that coveted slot in TV scheduling (New Year's Day), viewing figures peaked at a hefty 9.7 million in the first five minutes, rising to nearly 12 million once catch-up TV and on-demand services were factored in.

The episode was certainly well received by the *Mirror*, who awarded it an impressive five out of five stars. As for the big reveal, their verdict was as follows: 'The stunning explanation [. . .] for how Sherlock faked his death won't satisfy everybody, but it works.' The UK broadsheets were equally enthusiastic,

> **'I am so ready to play a really dumb character.'**
>
> *– Benedict Cumberbatch*

with the *Guardian*'s Sam Wollaston hailing it as 'an explosive return for Cumberbatch and Freeman; full of fizz, whizz and wit.'

Certain viewers were more hung up about the continuity, however. 'The Empty Hearse' is a largely underground-centric episode. Yet, as a disgruntled Anne-Marie Senior commented in the *Mirror*: '*Sherlock* sparks Twitter fury as eagle-eyed viewers notice the lines on London Underground are WRONG.' Oh dear. Come on, MoffGat, that's not exactly Sherlockian attention to detail now, is it? (Unless, of course, this was all deliberate: a coded clue to something momentous which will be explained in season four? That must be it. Sorry for doubting you, MoffGat.)

Fortunately this rail-related gaffe doesn't appear to have harmed the reputation of *Sherlock* over all. Cumberbitches have been particularly captivated by the intensifying SherWat love-in – with Holmes and Watson repeatedly declaring how much they mean to each other and how exceedingly deep their friendship runs. Aw . . . so, just how special is the bond that exists between Sherlock and his Watson? Viewers were falling over themselves to explore the question further via online fan fiction, many of them magnifying the homoerotic tension between John

Left: A family affair: Wanda Ventham and Timothy Carlton pictured with their other 'son' Mycroft (aka Mark Gatiss), at the IMAX 3D premiere of *Star Trek Into Darkness*. Right: Off to read some fan fiction? Benedict does dress-down Friday with Martin Freeman by his side, on the London set of *Sherlock*, August 2013.

and Sherlock well beyond what's shown onscreen – as B'batch himself is aware. In an interview with the *Sunday Times*, he commented that, 'there is weird fan fiction out there – weird. [. . .] They write stories and do manga cartoons of what they think you get up to behind closed doors. Some of it's funny. Some of it's full-on sex. Get Martin to show you some.'

Freeman added, 'There are a lot of people hoping that our characters and our selves are rampantly at it most of the time.' One person, however, who remains unsurprised by the world's obsession with Sherlock – and the men/women in his life – is Steven Moffat.

'Sherlock Holmes has always been a sex symbol [. . .] the most attractive person in the room is not always the best-looking; it's the most interesting.'

To Sherlock's chagrin, another recurring theme in season three is nepotism and/or family values (delete as appropriate, Sherfans, depending on your own personal POV). Wimothy deliver an adorable turn as Sherlock and Mycroft's dotty, musical-obsessed parents; Watson is suddenly all loved-up with Mary Morstan – played by the real-life Mrs M. Freeman, Amanda Abbington. Talk about keeping it in the family . . .

As any true Cumberfan can appreciate, *Sherlock* is ground-breaking for a number of reasons. It has: successfully updated the Most Famous Detective Ever, bringing him resoundingly into the 21st century; given us the incredibly versatile catch-phrase, 'did you miss me did you miss me did you miss me'; made geek the new chic and smart the new sexy; and – most importantly of all – introduced the universe to the super-star that is Benedict Cumberbatch (to say nothing of his accompanying Cumber-cheekbones). What's more, in late January 2014, the *Radio Times* explained that *Sherlock* 'has been officially announced as the [BBC's] most watched drama series in the UK since 2001, when the current ratings measurement system came in.' So it's official: not only is Benedict the king of the universe, the universe has become a Cumberverse. Bring on *Sherlock* season four. And five. (And six . . . and seven . . . and . . .)

AND THE OSCAR GOES TO . . .

Well, not to Benedict. Despite a host of nominations for *12 Years a Slave*, and a couple for *August: Osage County*, Benedict didn't get a look in at the 2014 Academy Awards. Or did he? In fact, according to basically everyone, he definitely scored the unofficial prize for Best Photobomb.

When Irish rock legends U2 – plus partners – lined up on the red carpet, little did they suspect that a bouncing Cumbercrasher was totally stealing their thunder by doing rock-star jumps behind them. Thanks to these pics, Benedict was splashed all over the internet, proving that you don't need a golden trophy to steal the show. (Though it's obviously only a matter of time before he pockets a few of them too.)

After bombing Bono and The Edge, Benedict himself became a red-carpet victim of photobombing while being interviewed about the success of *12 Years a Slave*. The *Daily Mail* reports how a mystery blonde in a very low-cut dress appeared behind the unsuspecting B'batch (where were his Sherlock reflexes?) and began rearranging her plunging neckline. Although the *Mail* reports that she got quite close and looked 'lovingly' towards Benedict, she somehow resisted touching his cheekbones. That's impressive self-control.

UP AND CUMBERING

We know there's more *Hobbit*-y goodness brewing – what with *The Hobbit: There and Back Again* opening *any second now* – and eventually we'll have season four of *Sherlock* to assuage our Cumber-cravings (do write faster, MoffGat), but in the meantime, where's our next fix of Benediction going to come from?

THE IMITATION GAME

Benedict stars in this biopic of Alan Turing, the brilliant mathematician-logician who was instrumental in cracking the Enigma code during World War Two (thus helping the allies defeat the Nazis). He was prosecuted for homosexuality in 1952 and sentenced to chemical castration. He killed himself two years later. Now, in the twenty-first century, Turing has received a posthumous Royal Pardon for his 'crime', but Benedict believes that – as homosexuality should

And the award for Best Thing Ever goes to … Benedict Cumberbatch at the 2014 Academy Awards. U2 rockers Bono and Larry Mullen, Jr were on the receiving end of this most epic of photobombs.

never be considered a crime – Turing has nothing to be pardoned for. Instead it is those who prosecuted him who should be asking for forgiveness. In an interview with *USA Today*, Benedict stated vehemently that, 'the only person that should be pardoning anybody is him. Hopefully, the film will bring to the fore what an extraordinary human

'I started preparing for *Hamlet* when I was seventeen. Probably before that.'

– *Benedict Cumberbatch*

being he was and how appalling [his treatment by the government was]. It's a really shameful, disgraceful part of our history.'

THE LOST CITY OF Z

Another biopic: this time centred round the life and times of 1920s British explorer Percy Fawcett (said to have inspired George Lucas's whip-cracking, thrill-seeking archaeologist, Indiana Jones), who became a laughing stock when he claimed to have discovered a hidden metropolis in the middle of the Amazon. In 1925 Fawcett and his son set out for the jungle – and were never heard of again . . . In the *Guardian*, Benedict describes Fawcett as, 'this rather brilliant, rather lovely Victorian man who just became obsessed with this discovery he made in the Amazon jungle.' For B'batch, portraying Fawcett onscreen is a fascinating prospect. As well as the fact that he was a friend of Arthur Conan Doyle's (#SherlockConnection), there's the draw of the mystery of his fate. As reported by the *Guardian*, 'What

'I just photo-Bono-bombed': Benedict looking pleased with himself at the Academy Awards, Hollywood, March 2014 – and rightly so.

happened to the adventurer remains one of the 20th century's enduring puzzles: an estimated 100 would-be-rescuers have died in more than thirteen expeditions (one as recently as 1996) sent to uncover Fawcett's fate.' For Cumberfans, the appeal is even less difficult to pinpoint. B'batch is obviously going to be looking super-stunning in those flapper-era khaki-coloured explorer hats.

HAMLET

Happily, Benedict's days of grabbing all the female roles are long over; so you can bet he won't be playing Ophelia in this, the most revered of all Shakespeare's plays. Instead he'll be taking on the great Dane (that's Hamlet, not the breed of dog), gracing the London stage as the prince-who's-haunted-by-his-father's-ghost-and-can't-decide-if-he-should-avenge-him-by-killing-his-murderous-uncle-who's-married-his-mother. When asked by *USA Today* if he was excited to be playing what is arguably the most famous part in the most famous play ever written, B'batch, unsurprisingly, said yes. 'Very excited. I don't know what other answer there would be to that question.'

CUMBERDREAMS

Take note casting directors – here are four roles that
Benedict simply needs to play.

God. With the recent spate of Bible flicks flooding our screens (Russell Crowe as Noah, Christian Bale as Moses ... So far Mel Gibson hasn't got involved, but give him time) it seems likely that there'll be some almighty Almighty portrayal coming up sometime soon. No offence to Alanis Morissette, who played the role of God in 1999's *Dogma* movie (the one which also casts Matt Damon and Ben Affleck as angels), but she seems nowhere near hyper enough to have created the earth. Bring on an energised Cumbergod at whose altar we all can worship ...

Withnail. To clarify, I do not think we need a remake of awesome 1987 classic *Withnail & I,* but as every successful (and some not-so-successful) film seems to be getting a reboot these days, it's surely best to prepare a strategy – especially one including Benedict as the hilarious, foul-mouthed, anxious drunkard-slash-failed-actor Withnail. Oh, and we already know how well he suits Withnail's long woollen coat.

Don Quixote. There is literally no one who I'd rather see fighting windmills. And obviously Martin Freeman could get in on the act as faithful sidekick Sancho Panza. The donkey would ideally be played by Donkey from *Shrek* (getting an American into the cast as a bonus). Not sure if long coats were in fashion in seventeenth-century Spain, but old Quixote was a bit ahead of his time in any case so I'm sure he could rock a Belstaff.

Inspector Gadget. Long face, long coat, a solution to every problem up his sleeve, his aptitude for flying ... you know this piece of casting makes sense. OK, granted Gadget isn't *quite* as sharp as Sherlock. But, nonetheless: 'Go go Benedict-Gadget movie!'

It's *au revoir, auf Wiedersehen,* see ya later, but never goodbye, Benedict – never goodbye. B'batch passes graciously down the red carpet at the 2014 SAG Awards, Los Angeles.

BENEDICT

CUMBERBATCH

British Library Cataloguing in Publication Data
A catalogue record for this book is available
from the British Library

ISBN-13: 978-0-85965-522-4

Cover photo by John Phillips/
UK Press/Getty Images
Printed in Great Britain by Bell & Bain Ltd

ACKNOWLEDGEMENTS

Benedict Cumberbatch has given interviews
to many newspapers, magazines and websites,
and these have proved invaluable in researching
this book. The author is particularly
indebted to the wonderfully comprehensive
Cumberbatchweb (benedictcumberbatch.
co.uk), as well as Caitlin Moran's illuminating
interview with Benedict for *The Times* from
May 2013. The author and editors would like
to give special thanks to: *The Guardian, The
Observer, The Telegraph, The Belfast Telegraph,
The Daily Mail, The Times, The Sunday Times,
The Metro, The Mirror, The Sun, The Independent,
The Independent on Sunday, The Radio Times,
Entertainment Weekly, USA Today, LA Times,
The Hollywood Reporter, The New York Times,
Herald Scotland, The Argus, The Huffington Post,
Elle, Esquire, Event Magazine, GQ, InStyle,
Interview Magazine, Now Magazine, Rolling Stone,
TV Times, Time Magazine, Vogue, The Graham
Norton Show, The Guinness Book of World
Records*, sherlockology.com, dramaticneed.org,
avclub.com, zap2it.com, dnaindia.com,
tvequals.com, cumberbatchfans.livejournal.com,
twitter.com, brambletye.co.uk, harrowschool.org.uk,
lamda.org.uk, bbc.co.uk, sky.com, imdb.com,
youtube.com, buzzfeed.com, denofgeek.com,
en.wikipedia.org, fz.com.

We would also like to thank the following
agencies for providing pictures: Rex; Rex/
ITV; Alex Macnaughton; Rex/Richard
Saker; Rex/Steve Clark; Rex/Simon
Runting; Rex/Snap Stills; Rex/Moviestore
Collection; Rex/c.Focus/Everett; Rex/
c.Newmarket/Everett; Rex/Nils Jorgensen;
Rex/Richard Young; Rex/Alastair Muir;
Rex/c.HBO/Everett; Rex/Jim Smeal/BEI;
Rex/Paramount Pictures/courtesy Everett
Collection; Rex/c.Touchstone/Everett;
Rex/c.FoxSearch/Everett; Didier Messens/
Getty Images; Mike Marsland/ Wire Image:
Getty Images; Ben Pruchnie/Getty Images;
Dave Hogan/Getty Images; Tony Barson
Archive/Wire Image: Getty Images; Stephen
Shugerman/Getty Images; Dave M. Benett/
Getty Images; Jon Furniss/Wire Image:
Getty Images; Vittorio Zunino Celotto/
Getty Images; Max Mumby/Indigo/Getty
Images; Matthew Lloyd/Getty Images;
Toronto Star via Getty Images; Charley
Gallay/Getty Images for Vanity Fair; Larry
Busacca/Getty Images; Mark Robert
Milan/Film Magic; Kevork Djansezian/
Getty Images; benedictcumberbatch.co.uk;
whatareyouwearingbenedict.tumblr.com;
Image Net; Kevin Winter/Image Net; Stuart
C. Wilson/Image Net; Gareth Cattermole/
Image Net; Ken Ishii/Image Net; Mirrorpix.
Every effort has been made to trace copyright
holders. The publishers would be pleased
to rectify any unintentional omission in
subsequent printings.